Also by Patrick F. McManus

Never Cry "Arp!"

How I Got This Way

The Good Samaritan Strikes Again

Whatchagot Stew (with Patricia M. Gass)

Real Ponies Don't Go Oink

The Night the Bear Ate Goombaw

Rubber Legs and White Tail-Hairs

The Grasshopper Trap

Never Sniff a Gift Fish

They Shoot Canoes, Don't They?

Kid Camping from Aaaaiii! to Zip

A Fine and Pleasant Misery

Into the Twilight, Endlessly Grousing

Patrick F. McManus

A Fireside Book
Published by Simon & Schuster

FIRESIDE
Rockefeller Center
1230 Avenue of the Americas
New York, NY 10020

First Fireside Edition 1998

FIRESIDE and colophon are registered trademarks
of Simon & Schuster Inc.

Designed by Sam Potts
Manufactured in the United States of America
1   3   5   7   9   10   8   6   4   2

The Library of Congress has cataloged
the Simon & Schuster edition as follows:
McManus, Patrick F.
Into the twilight, endlessly grousing /
Patrick F. McManus.
p.   cm.
1. American wit and humor. I. Title.
PN6162.M34896   1997
813'.54—dc21   97-23502
CIP
ISBN 0-684-84440-0
0-684-84799-X (pbk)

Permissions appear on page 221.

Contents

INTO
THE
TWILIGHT,
ENDLESSLY
GROUSING

The Boy

Sometimes I'd take the boy fishing. He was not my boy but somebody else's, and that was good, his appetite and the cost of food being what they were. Mostly, I used him to hold down the bow of my canoe, instead of the bags of lead shot I usually employed for that purpose. He was smarter than the lead shot but not so much you would notice.

"I wonder what causes the tides," he said once.

"The moon," I told him.

"The moon!" he cried, doubling over with laughter. "You expect me to believe that? You must think I'm stupid!"

I treated myself to a thoughtful pause.

"The earth is round," I said.

"So?" he said. "Everybody knows that."

"Just checking," I said.

The boy was about sixteen that year, the year I used him for lead shot. Whenever he ran out of money, which was often, he would come over to my cabin on the river and work for me. Mostly, I would have him dig holes in the ground. When you own a cabin on a river, you always have need for lots of holes in the ground. I enjoyed listening to him complain about the pay, because then I knew I wasn't paying him too much. I prefer to err on the side of not enough, because it is wrong to spoil youngsters by paying them too much.

Whenever he complained about the pay, I would tell him about my first job. I was fourteen and worked for a farmer all one summer digging holes in the ground. The farmer was so cruel and sadistic that he had probably once been a commandant in charge of a slave labor camp. But I was the only one who suspected his previous employment. Everyone else thought he was a fair and decent and good-hearted man. But they didn't dig holes for him.

"Vork! Vork!" the farmer would scream at me.

About once a week I would get mad and resign my position. Then the farmer would come and tell my mother what a fine worker I was and that he wanted me back to dig more holes. He told her that my work habits had improved greatly under his supervision, and now my pace was such that he could often detect movement with the naked eye. So Mom would make me go back to digging holes.

"Vork! Vork!" the farmer would scream.

By the end of summer, I hadn't earned quite enough money to buy my first deer rifle. The farmer gave me a bonus to make up the difference! I was astounded. Furthermore, I became the only person he would let hunt deer on his property, because I had been such a good and loyal worker and also because there were no deer there.

"So," I said to the boy, "do you see the moral to this story?"

"No," he said. "It's a boring story and I don't want to hear it ever again."

"Vork! Vork!" I shouted at him.

Sometimes, when the fishing was good, I would go out in the canoe almost every morning. I would get up very early and rush down to the river still buttoning my shirt, but the boy would be there already, waiting. I suspected he slept in the canoe, just so I couldn't slip away without him. We would paddle off to fish the channels that flowed between the islands where the river merged with the lake. As we paddled along we would exchange our theories about the purpose of human life. My theory was that the purpose of life was to perfect ourselves through learning and discipline in order to fulfill our cosmic responsibilities as part of the self-consciousness of the universe. He thought the purpose of human life was for him to buy a car.

At the beginning of summer, the boy knew nothing about fishing, but by July he knew everything and had begun to advise me.

"That fly you're tying on is too big," he'd say. "Better go to a sixteen. And switch to a black gnat."

"How do you know all this?" I said.

"It's easy," he said. "I think like a fish."

"I can't argue with that," I said.

He enjoyed teasing me, because now he almost always caught more fish than I did. I would chuckle good-naturedly, swack the water just so with the paddle, and soak him to the skin.

The boy had a talent for getting on my nerves. I could remember how peaceful it had once been, when I was a solitary paddler, slipping quietly along the channels between the islands, doing everything just right, becoming one with nature and the mosquitoes and deerflies. But now the boy was always there, yakking, advising me on fishing technique, philosophizing about cars, complaining about the lunch I'd brought along and the pay he was getting for digging holes.

And then one morning he wasn't waiting for me at the canoe. He didn't come the next morning either. Or the following week. It was a relief. I was glad to be rid of him. Having nothing else to do, I asked around about him the next time I was in town. Most folks had no idea who he was, but the lady who runs the grocery said she thought he lived out on such-and-such road. Still having nothing else to do, I drove out the road and found an ancient mobile home approaching terminal depreciation, under some scraggly pines. No one was home. A man stood watching me over a nearby fence.

"They's gone," he said. "Just packed up and left one day. Headed for Oklahoma. I'm from Oklahoma myself."

"Oklahoma," I said. "Any fishing there?"

"Good fishin'."

"I'm glad to hear it."

I went out fishing the next morning but it wasn't the same. A boy works a whole lot better than bags of lead shot for holding down the bow of a canoe, no question about it.

About a week later, another boy showed up at my cabin, apparently having heard I was short a boy. He was a redheaded kid with glasses that kept slipping down his freckled nose.

"I hear you got some work here," he said.

"I do," I said.

"What's the pay?"

I told him. He managed to stifle any hint of elation.

"What's the work?"

"I got all these holes I need filled up."

"I guess I can do that." He watched me for a moment, pushing his glasses back up his freckled nose. "What you doin' there to your canoe?"

"Nothing much," I said. "Just removing some bags of lead shot from the bow."

Mountain Men

After hours of prospecting highway ditches, Crazy Eddie Muldoon and I hit the mother lode of empties. We had been working the ditches along the highway, picking up singles here and there and the occasional double. At half a cent a beer bottle, though, we were still well short of the eighteen cents we'd need for two tickets to the Saturday matinee, to say nothing of five cents each for popcorn. Then Eddie came up with one of his fabulous ideas.

"I got an idea, Pat. Let's go check out Lovers Leap. It's a parking place up on top of Nob Hill."

"Lovers Leap?" I said. "I wonder why they call it Lovers Leap."

"Don't you know nothin', Pat? Lovers go up there to leap off."

"You mean they kill themselves!"

"The leap ain't that high. I 'spect about all they'd do is break a leg."

"Lovers must be pretty strange."

"Yeah. Love drives 'em crazy. Good thing you and me are going to be mountain men. We won't have to put up with all that dumb love stuff."

Fortunately, there were no lovers at Lovers Leap when we arrived, although neither Eddie nor I would have minded seeing one or two of them fly off into space. What we did find were dozens of beer bottles scattered all over the place. Eddie said maybe the lovers didn't leap from the knob at all. Maybe they just got drunk and fell off.

After filling our gunnysacks with empties and loading the sacks on Eddie's wagon, we still had enough time to exchange our loot for hard cash and make it to the Saturday matinee if we hurried. The two-mile hike to town was hot and dusty, and by the time we came to Pig Weed's Saloon, we were dying of thirst. The sounds of laughter and honky-tonk music drifted out, beckoning in the sinful.

"Sounds like the folks in Pig Weed's are having a good time," Eddie said.

"My mom says all kinds of evil stuff goes on in there," I said.

"You ever seen any evil, Pat?"

"Naw. You?"

"Nope. Boy, Ma would tan me good if she ever caught me in Pig Weed's Saloon."

"Mine, too!"

Jake was tending the bar when we hauled our wagon through the saloon's swinging doors. "Hey, if it ain't Pat and Eddie!"

We parked our wagon and climbed up on bar stools.

"Hi, Jake," Eddie said. "We brought you some more empties."

"I can see that. Looks like you hit the jackpot this time. What'll it be, boys?"

"The usual, Jake," I said.

"Let's see, that's two double shots of whiskey with beer chasers, as I recall."

"You bet," Eddie said.

Jake reached into a cooler, hauled out two icy bottles of Orange Crush, and set them on the bar in front of us. "It's on the house."

"Thanks, Jake."

Miz Weed came out of her office smoking a cigar. "Oh *bleep!*" she rasped. "Not you two twerps again! Pat and Eddie, how many times I got to tell you, sell your empties someplace else! Your mothers would skin both you and me alive, they ever catch you in here."

"Oh, you don't have to worry, Miz Weed," Eddie said. "Mom says she'd never set foot in this 'pit of sin.'"

"Is that right, Eddie? Your mom said 'pit of sin'?"

"Yep. So don't you worry about her showing up. Anyway, Jake gives us the best price for our empties."

Jake put a finger to his lips and shook his head.

"I bet he does," Miz Weed said. "Jake's mighty generous with my money. Well, finish your pops, and then scat! This pit of sin ain't no place for two seven-year-old boys."

"Gee, Miz Weed," I said. "If you're afraid of us seeing some evil, neither Eddie nor I would mind a bit."

The way she rolled her eyes up toward the ceiling, I could see Miz Weed was giving my comment some serious consideration, but at that very moment the swinging doors burst open with a bang and a rattle. The joyous ruckus of the saloon died an instant death. Jake's jaw sagged. Every head swiveled toward the intruder. Eddie and I wheeled around on our stools.

Looming there in the doorway stood the most frightening figure I'd ever seen or even imagined. He was tall and lean, with a huge hawkish nose and a shaggy mustache that drooped down past the edges of a grim mouth. Mean little eyes squinted out from beneath bushy eyebrows. Rivers of sweat had cut little channels down his face through what appeared to be a crust composed of dirt, smoke, grit, and the odd flying insect. Escaping from beneath a broad-brimmed hat, gray-streaked hair hung down almost to his shoulders. Grease and grime coated his buckskin shirt, and from his belt hung the largest knife I'd ever seen. In one hand he carried a rifle.

Behind us, Jake mumbled, "I can see this ain't gonna be one of my better days."

After glancing about the room to make sure everyone was properly terrified, the man strode up to the bar right next to Eddie and me. He laid the rifle on the bar within easy reach, probably just in case some fool might have an attack of lunacy and cause him a bit of annoyance.

"Whiskey!" he growled.

"Yes sir!" Jake set a shot glass of whiskey in front of him.

"You call thet whiskey!" The man picked up his rifle and swept the glass off the bar with it.

"What am I thinking of!" Jake set the bottle on the bar. The man tilted up the bottle and chugalugged a goodly portion. Then he growled at Jake, "Now get me some pliers."

"Pliers! Pliers!" Jake croaked, rummaging about under the bar. "We got some here someplace. Hope we got some. Don't have much call for . . . Ah! Here they are!"

The man grabbed the pliers, opened his craterous mouth, and stuck the pliers back in so far they must have touched his tonsils. He then clamped down and began wrenching on the pliers, all the while making the most terrible, ghastly, sickening sounds I'd ever heard. And then he hauled out a massive tooth and flung it on the bar in front of Jake.

"Thar, gol-dang ya!" he said to the tooth. "You and me is parted company. Let thet be a lesson to you, causin' me thet kinda misery."

He spat a glob of blood on the floor, took another gulp of whiskey, plunked a silver dollar on the bar, picked up the bottle and his rifle, glanced about the room one more time to make sure everyone was behaving himself, and strode out the door.

The collective sigh of relief heaved by the saloon's patrons rattled the windows. Thinking I might have just witnessed some evil, I turned to Jake. He was mopping sweat off his forehead with a bar towel. "What was that?"

"That, Patrick, was a mountain man, somehow left over from history."

"Gee, a real mountain man!" Eddie said.

"As real as you could find nowadays, I reckon," Jake said. "This here was only the second time I ever seen him. He burst in here one night a couple years ago and roared out at somebody, 'Now I got you, you no-good thievin' rat!' Well, half the boys in here fit that description, and they jumped up and run out the back door. Don't know if he ever did catch the feller he was after. If he did catch him, I don't imagine there was much reason to wait breakfast on him in the morning."

"Cripes, Jake," I said. "Where does the mountain man live anyway?"

"Oh, I think he mostly roams the mountains, but I understand he's got a little cabin up Trapper Crick. Course, nobody in his right mind ever goes up there. If he does, I don't reckon he comes back. So I'm not sure about the cabin."

Miz Weed, who had been rushing about throwing open all the windows, suddenly noticed us again. She wasn't too pleased, or so I judged from the really bad word she blurted out. "You twerps got exactly thirty seconds to get your business done with Jake and your butts outta here!"

"Gee whiz, Miz Weed, we—"

"Twenty-five seconds!"

Jake grabbed the mountain man's dollar off the bar and handed it to us. "You boys git."

"But, Jake, you didn't even count the empties!"

"Yep, I did," he whispered. "Got X-ray vision can see right through those ole gunnysacks. Come out a dollar even."

"Wow, a whole dollar!" Eddie cried. "Thanks, Jake!"

"Not so loud," Jake said, glancing over at Miz Weed, who paused from counting off seconds to glare at her bartender.

We set the sacks on the floor, grabbed the wagon, and headed for the door. Jake's X-ray vision wasn't all that good. There wasn't more than twenty cents' worth of empties in those sacks. Sometimes we felt bad about taking advantage of Jake, but the feeling never lasted long enough to make a nuisance of itself.

At the door, Eddie suddenly stopped and turned. "What's that mountain man's name anyway, Jake?"

"Crabtree," Jake said. "Rancid is what folks call him. Rancid Crabtree."

"*Rancid* Crabtree? How come they call him Rancid?"

"You got a cold, Eddie?" Jake said. "You didn't smell nothin'?"

We sniffed. Why yes, a pungent odor still lingered in the air, even after the brisk breeze Miz Weed had let in through the windows.

"You're right," Eddie said. "I guess I was too scared to smell when we were at the bar with him and you."

Jake gave us a crazed look. "Just as well, I'd say," he grunted, tossing back a shot of whiskey. "You boys don't get any of your weird ideas, hear? You'll steer clear of Crabtree, if you know what's good for you!"

Eddie and I plodded off toward town and the matinee, both of us enjoying the warm and satisfying feeling that comes from sudden wealth. With a whole dollar, we could buy out half the town. We could buy *real estate,* if we had any use for it.

"Hold up a sec," Eddie said. He pointed far off to a thickly forested area between two mountains. "You know what? Trapper Crick flows out of there."

"So?" I said, reluctantly distracted from contemplating the purchasing potential of our dollar.

"Well, I was just thinking," Eddie said. "Maybe we should sneak up there, find Crabtree's cabin, and spy on him. Maybe we could see him do some mountain man stuff. Maybe he'd shoot a bear or something. What do you think?"

"Didn't you hear what Jake said about Crabtree, Eddie? Anybody who goes up there probably doesn't come back."

"Oh, you know what a kidder Jake is. How about it?"

"Sounds okay to me," I said. "I'll tell you what, you can sneak up and spy on Crabtree while I stand watch."

"I was kinda thinking we'd do it the other way around," Eddie said. "Where was you thinking you'd stand watch?"

"Right about here," I said. "But maybe not quite this close."

Before spying on Crabtree, we had to wait a few days for the image of the fierce old mountain man to fade below our terror threshold. Most of our adventures resulted from our level of boredom rising above our level of fear. One morning when we had nothing else to do but sit on the Muldoon corral fence and use ourselves as bait for mosquitoes, Eddie determined that his boredom had just about reached critical mass. "We've waited long enough. Let's go spy on Crabtree."

"Geez, Eddie, I don't know," I said, wiping out three mosquitoes on my arm with one swat. "I'm not that bored yet. Besides, if old Crabtree catches us, he might kill us."

"Of course he'll kill us, Pat, if he catches us. That's what mountain men do when they catch somebody spying on them. But he ain't going to catch us."

"Yeah but—"

"C'mon, you can't chicken out on me now. Don't you want to be a mountain man?"

"Sure."

"See, we can spy on old Crabtree and learn how to do all kinds of mountain man stuff. It'll save us a whole bunch of time if we don't have to learn it all on our own. Otherwise, we'll be stuck in school practically forever."

Eddie was right, I could see that. The faster we learned how to be mountain men, the sooner we could leave school, go off into the wilderness, and live off the land. Second grade had been a terrible bore the previous year. And it wasn't one bit better *this* year! Right now it looked as if I might never get out of second grade.

"You're right, Eddie. Let's go."

"Great! But we better tell Ma and Pa first."

"Why tell them, Eddie? They'll probably just get all nervous and shaky like always and then tell us we can't go, because it's too dangerous."

"I know, but I don't like them to worry. You don't say nothin', okay? I'll handle this."

Both of Eddie's parents seemed to suffer from some kind of nervous disorder. In fact, Mr. Muldoon's face would begin to twitch every time he saw Eddie and me together, and Mrs. Muldoon would wring her hands and sometimes even chew on a fingernail. I'd told Eddie I thought maybe his folks had some kind of strange disease, but he said he was pretty sure their nervous condition was just a result of drinking too much coffee. "Coffee's awful bad for the nerves," he'd explained.

Both Eddie's parents were in the kitchen when we burst in on them.

"Good cripes!" Mr. Muldoon yelped, frantically brushing spilled hot coffee off his pants. "How many times I got to tell you boys, walk through the door just as if you was regular human beings. You don't have to take it off the hinges!"

"Sorry, Pa," Eddie said. "Anyway, I just want to let you know Pat and I are going on a hike."

"A hike?" Mrs. Muldoon said, chewing a fingernail.

"You're not taking any of my tools, are you?" Mr. Muldoon said. "You boys stay away from my tools. I don't want you chopping down any more trees, or building deep-sea-diving outfits with my milk buckets, or building airplanes on top of the barn roof, or digging pit traps in the pasture to capture wild animals, or starting campfires, or—"

"Naw, we're just going on a hike, Pa."

Mr. Muldoon's face twitched. "Well, I guess there isn't too much harm in that. For gosh sakes, just don't build nothin'!"

"Lord save us, *no!*" Mrs. Muldoon cried, wringing her hands. "And don't build any more rafts out of fence posts! You'll drown for sure."

"That's right," Mr. Muldoon said. "Besides, I need all the fence posts I got left!"

"You make sure your hike doesn't take you anywhere near that pit of sin, Pig Weed's Saloon," Mrs. Muldoon said.

"We won't go near Pig Weed's," Eddie said. "We'll stay clear of that evil place."

"Well," Mrs. Muldoon said, "I guess I could make you a sack lunch for your little hike."

"Oh," Mr. Muldoon said, "and no more snares! The last one I caught my foot in nearly broke my leg. Can you think of anything else, Sarah?" His face twitched again.

"It's just so hard to cover everything, Herb. It's just so hard."

Eddie was probably right. His folks must have drunk way too much coffee.

An hour later, Eddie and I were working our way up the Trapper Creek trail. The trail was overgrown with brush on both sides and obviously didn't get much use.

"Remember what Jake said?" I asked Eddie. "How he suspected that anybody that came up Trapper Creek probably didn't come back?"

"Yeah, I been thinking about that. Maybe we shouldn't stick to the trail. Let's cut up over that ridge. We might be able to see Crabtree's cabin from there."

We crossed a log over the creek and climbed up to the ridge. Sure enough, tucked away in a clearing down below was a little cabin. Eddie and I lay down side by side so we could just peek over the rocky lip of the ridge. An overgrown logging road entered the clearing from the far side, and at the end of the road an ancient truck rusted its way toward oblivion. All kinds of interesting junk was strewn about among tall weeds: a set of bedsprings, part of a milk separator, a broken table, a gas tank, a wheel from a hay wagon, and dozens of things we couldn't even recognize. And then there were the bones, gleaming whitely in the sun.

"Any of those bones look human to you?" I whispered to Eddie.

"Most of them," Eddie whispered back. "I don't see no human skulls, though. He probably keeps a collection of them in his cabin. I reckon old Crabtree just tosses his victims out in the yard after he kills them."

"Geez!" I whispered. "Let's get out of here!"

"Don't worry, Pat, he won't ever spot us up here. Besides, we want to see him do some mountain man stuff."

We lay there for what seemed like hours without catching a glimpse of Crabtree. Wisps of smoke drifted up out of the stone chimney, so we were pretty sure he was home. Then I noticed a faint odor. It seemed to be growing stronger.

"You smell that, Eddie?"

"Yeah. It's pretty awful."

"What do you suppose it is?"

"I don't know. Maybe Crabtree is burning some rotten old hides in his stove."

"It keeps getting stronger."

"Wind must have shifted and be blowing the smoke up here."

The hair on the back of my neck lifted. My hair was always a pretty good detector of danger. "I'm getting a little scared, Eddie. Something doesn't feel right."

"Y-yeah. Uh, I don't want you to get too scared, Pat. We b-b-better head on home."

I started to push back from the ledge but my feet bumped into a rock. I moved my feet to one side to get around it. But the rock moved, too. This seemed a rather bad omen. I turned and looked up. Towering over us was—Rancid Crabtree!

What happened next was all kind of a blur. I do recall being snatched up by the back of my shirt, and I had this image of Eddie's legs running like crazy but unable to get any traction because they were way up in the air. And then something was pulled over my head and I was flipped upside down. The next thing I knew, I was being bounced along on Crabtree's shoulder like a bag of grain. At one point I was dropped on the ground. I heard a paper sack being opened and then the rustle of waxed paper followed by chewing sounds. Crabtree was eating our lunch! Then I was hoisted back up and carted off again. Finally, I was dropped on a hard surface of some kind. All this while I'd tried to keep my breathing to a minimum so as not to call attention to myself, but now I stopped breathing altogether and listened for sounds of Crabtree. Silence. The odor was fading. The murderous old mountain man had probably left me in one of his secret places, intending to come back later and finish me off. And then I heard a muffled cry from Eddie.

"Help!"

A door opened.

"Help!"

"For heaven's sakes!" Mrs. Muldoon said. "What are you boys doing in those gunnysacks! How in the world? Why, the sacks are tied shut! And here's a note! I can barely make it out. Let's see: 'Keep . . . these . . . younguns out of my . . . hair . . . or else! Yours truly . . . Rancid Crabtree. P.S. Thanks for . . . the lunch!' My goodness, what terrible spelling."

"Forget the spelling, Ma," Eddie said. "Get us out of these sacks."

Mrs. Muldoon seemed to be thinking about what to do next. "Oh, I will, Eddie, I will. But first I think I'll make myself a nice cup of tea, put my feet up, and treat myself to a little peace and quiet." The door closed.

"Geez, I don't know what gets into Ma," Eddie said. "Well, I'll tell you one thing, Pat. Next time old Crabtree won't find us so easy to catch."

"Next time! What do you mean, next time, Eddie? He catches us again, he'll kill us for sure!"

"Naw, this is great. See, if he was going to kill us, he'd have killed us this time. Instead, he just hauled us back home. He ain't as fierce as everybody thinks."

"Yeah, well, next time you go without me."

"C'mon, Pat, don't you want to learn to be a mountain man? You want to spend the rest of your life in second grade?"

One thing about Eddie, he knew how to push all the right buttons.

As punishment for "tormenting" Rancid Crabtree, both Crazy Eddie and I were placed under house arrest for a whole week. Talk about your miscarriage of justice. You'd think we'd stuck Crabtree in a gunnysack and kidnapped *him!*

Under the terms of our parole the following week, Eddie and I were forbidden to associate with any dangerous and unsavory characters—namely each other—for an unspecified period of time. So our only means of communication was Morse code, blinked with flashlights at night across the fields between our homes. One night Eddie blinked out this message to me: C-T-H-L-T-M-E-S-N-I-B. I blinked back a terse reply: B-I-P-F-O-G. As Eddie often pointed out, one of these days we'd actually have to learn Morse code. That way the message wouldn't always have to be the same: "Meet me at the Big Tree."

I slipped out my bedroom window and ran to the Big Tree, a solitary cottonwood in the middle of our hay field. Eddie was already there.

"I got our next raid on old Crabtree all worked out," he said.

"What raid? You know we're not supposed to bother Crabtree anymore."

"Us bother him? He's the one tied us up in gunnysacks and carted us home like a couple weaner pigs. It was just like he kidnapped us, and our folks didn't even call the sheriff on him or nothin'. Shucks, I even heard Pa say he wished he'd come up with that gunnysack idea. Nope, we got to take revenge on Crabtree ourselves."

"Revenge? Eddie, don't you understand? That old mountain man will kill us just for showing up, let alone us trying to take revenge on him."

"Well, not revenge really. What we'll do is set a trap for him. See, I got it all drawn out here." He turned his flash-light on a sheet of tablet paper. "This here is a wild-animal pit trap, just like the one we caught Pa in."

"Eddie, besides your pa, all we ever caught in that trap was a little skunk."

"Well, they was both wild, wasn't they? Pa in particu-lar. Now, with this other trap, see, we bend a tree over and tie a snare on the end of it. When Crabtree steps in the snare, he gets jerked way up in the air. I seen it done in a movie and it worked great."

"Eddie, we've never caught anything in a snare, either. Well, sure, your pa, but he's easy—he isn't a mountain man. Mountain men know all about snares and are watching out for them. Besides, what would we do with Crabtree after we caught him?"

"You're so dumb sometimes, Pat. The whole idea is, we don't release him until he promises to teach us how to be mountain men."

"I don't know, it sounds awfully dangerous to me, Eddie."

"Yeah, don't it! I can't wait!"

It took us several days to get our traps set for the moun-tain man. The tricky part was coming up with the bait for luring Crabtree into our traps. But at last we were ready.

Crouched in the woods at the edge of Crabtree's clear-ing, we waited for him to emerge from his cabin.

"I always thought mountain men got up at the crack of dawn," Eddie said. "It's already almost noon. Oh, look, he's coming out."

Crabtree strolled from his cabin, stretching and yawning. Suddenly, he stopped and glanced about, as if his keen mountain man senses detected intruders nearby. Then he reached down and picked up the note Eddie had left on his chopping block. The note said: "We've come for our revenge, Mr. Crabtree. If you know what's good for you, you'll surrender. We're waiting for you on the trail. Eddie and Pat."

Eddie nudged me in the ribs. "I bet he'll get a big kick out of our note. Any second now he'll burst out laughing."

The mountain man wadded up the note, threw it on the ground, jerked his ax from the chopping block, and came striding right toward us.

"Then again, maybe not."

Forsaking dignity for haste, we retreated to our observation post up the hill on the far side of the creek. It was pretty clear Eddie had been wrong about Crabtree. He was just as dangerous and crazy as we'd been told. We watched as he approached our snare. Suddenly he stopped and peered at the ground ahead of him.

"A peanut butter and jelly sandwich!" he roared, glaring this way and that into the woods. "You miserable little tadpoles thank a peanut butter and jelly sandwich is any way to bait a snare fer me? It's a gol-dang insult, thet's what it is! And Ah s'pose you thank thet puny tree you bent over is gonna snatch me up in the air? Wahl, Ah'll show you somethin'! Ah'm gonna jump right in the middle of your snare and squish thet sandwich flat!"

He put his feet together and hopped into the middle of the snare.

"Gollll-dannnnnggg!"

"It worked!" Eddie cried.

"Wow, neato!" I said. "That was a really great idea, Eddie, hiding the pit trap under the snare!"

We raced down to the pit and peeked over the edge. Crabtree sat in the dirt at the bottom. He glared up at us.

"We got you now, Mr. Crabtree," Eddie told him.

"Looks thet way," Crabtree growled. "You done fooled me. Ah surrenders."

"Good," Eddie said. "I hope you didn't get hurt."

"Nope. Jist skeered me a bit. Fer a second thar when Ah was droppin', it flashed through maw mind you might've put sharpened stakes in the bottom of the pit."

"Oh, we wouldn't do that," I said.

"Naw," Eddie added. "We didn't want to kill you. That way you wouldn't be able to teach us how to be mountain men."

"Mighty kind of you. Now, what's this about me teachin' you to be mountain men? What's them?"

"Well, like you are. We want to be just like you."

"You *do?* Wahl, thet's the fust time Ah ever heard thet from anybody!"

"See," Eddie explained, "we want you to teach us how to hunt and trap and fish and how to live off the land like you do."

"Ah guess thet won't be too hard, larnin' to live off the land. Fust thang you gots to do is get yourselves the right tool."

"Great! What's that?"

"A can opener! Ah can teach you somethin' about pit traps, too."

"Really?"

"Yep. You gots to dig them deeper." Crabtree stood up. The top of the pit trap came only to his waist.

"Oh, that," Eddie said, a bit miffed at the criticism.

"Well, we didn't want you to break a leg or nothin'."

"Downright thoughtful of you."

"We got tired of digging, too," I said.

"Thet's what Ah figured," Crabtree said, climbing out of our trap. "So you pups wants to be jist like me. Mebby you two ain't so bad after all. Ah likes to see thet kind of ambition in a couple younguns. But it ain't gonna be easy. We can start right now. Fust thang you do is go dig me some worms, so Ah can catch me some fish fer breakfast. Then Ah got to go lay down and rest. Ain't used to all this excitement so early in the mornin'."

Rancid kept his word, too. Over the years that followed, he taught us everything he knew. But it wasn't enough. Much to my regret, we never did get to become mountain men.

Smoke!

For more than thirty years, I carried on a love affair with—how shall I put it?—an object of my affection. But my wife, Bun, intolerant of such matters, finally issued an ultimatum. "Get rid of that sop or else!" she said, without bothering to mince a single word. "Sop," S.O.P., was her abbreviation for "stinky old pipe."

There were a couple of dozen sops in my life, all loved passionately, but Bun always referred to the many as if they were one. That pipe! That stinky old pipe! In regard to the word "stinky," I must point out that "stink" is a relative term. What is stink to one person is heavenly aroma to another, particularly a pipe smoker or, possibly, a junk-yard dog, whose discriminating tastes some think I share.

What has got me to thinking about pipes today is that I have just read *The Ultimate Pipe Book* by Richard Carleton Hacker. True, Mr. Hacker does have an unfortunate last name for the author of a book on pipe smoking, but it is his real name, and he is not about to conceal it behind a sissy pseudonym merely to escape an irony. Mr. Hacker is a fine writer and writes of pipes with a devotion that can be appreciated only by a person of great passions, namely a pipe smoker, past or present.

I don't know Mr. Hacker, but I imagine him in a smoking jacket, seated in a paneled, book-lined study, puffing contentedly away on an elegant briar or meerschaum as he pens his next scholarly work on, yes, pipes. His thoughts and the aroma of his English tobacco blend as one as he searches through his vast reservoir of knowledge on the culture and history of pipes and pipe tobaccos, seeking that next perfect but elusive sentence. Well, I, too, have a pipe history, and I hereby offer it up to Mr. Hacker to add to his next tome, should he so choose.

My introduction to smoking occurred at age seven. Crazy Eddie Muldoon and I had pursued our innocent hobby of collecting cigarette butts from along the highway for several months, with no particular use for them in mind. Then one day it occurred to us, like a bolt out of the blue, that we might actually *smoke* the butts! We had stored them in, appropriately, a cigar box. When we had accumulated a sufficient supply, namely a full cigar box, we went up on the mountain near our homes, found comfortable seats on the edge of a rock cliff, and gazing happily out over the checkerboard landscape below, smoked up almost our entire collection in about an hour, although the amount of elapsed time is rather vague to me now (as it was then, for that matter). I don't know about Eddie, but as for myself, I never again smoked a cigarette, nor have I had any desire to do so. Perhaps it was because of the odd sensation of having an ice pick driven through my head from one temple to the other. Or perhaps it was fright over the pale, greenish blur that had become Eddie's face, as he lay on his back moaning something about his imminent death, thereby removing from the realm of idle speculation my last doubt that my own demise was close at hand. I will spare the reader graphic details of our illness, except to mention in a general way that four or five times we were turned inside out and back again. Eddie went home in such a confused state that he forgot to get himself turned right side out and gave his parents a tremendous shock. (There's nothing more disgusting than an inside-out person.) As for myself, anytime I was jostled during the next week, a little puff of smoke went up.

I took up pipe smoking, at age twenty-four, mostly for the sake of appearance. Even Bun said the pipe gave me a look of scholarly distinction. It was fortunate that it did, because shortly after taking up the pipe I was hired as an instructor at a university. Looking back, I believe that the chairman of the English Department must have hired me solely on the basis that I smoked a pipe, for that was about my only qualification. The chairman smoked a pipe, too. A distinguished scholar himself, he must have felt that my pipe was evidence of great but as of yet undetectable professorial potential. The pipe carried me all the way through to full professorhood, without anyone ever discovering the truth. Oh sure, there were suspicions, but nothing was ever proved.

In addition to contributing to success in one's career, the pipe is a wonderful instrument for the enhancement of fishing. It is an especially useful accessory for fly-fishing, in that its mere presence in the mouth suggests to one's fellow anglers an easy competence. Even though my own fly casting has been said to resemble an old lady fighting off a bee with a broom handle, I discovered that merely by my hauling out a pipe, lighting up, and puffing out great clouds of smoke, other anglers on the stream were instantly impressed and would begin asking technical questions of me. Oh, not about fly-fishing, but other things, such as did I know who hit the most home runs in the 1952 World Series, stuff like that. I suppose they might even have asked me about fly-fishing, except for my occasionally getting my pipe caught in the line. I once cast one of my favorite briars halfway across the Madison River and received a round of applause from the other anglers, but that is something that shouldn't be attempted by beginners. Practice at home first.

Not all of my experiences with pipes were so pleasant. One time my nephew Shaun bought a new motorcycle and offered me a ride. Chuckling as I ignited a fresh pipeful of tobacco, I declined, mostly for the reason that Shaun had a long history of luring me into serious predicaments. When he was about age ten, for example, he persuaded me to take him fishing on a stream not far from his home. It was late in the season and I knew that the stream would have been heavily fished and was not likely to produce a strike, let alone a fish. Mostly to silence his pleading, I drove Shaun up to the stream. Much to my surprise, both he and I caught big fat rainbows on our first few casts.

"Wow!" I exclaimed. "This is terrific, Shaun! I can't believe the fishing is so good here this late in the season! It's amazing this stream hasn't been fished out by now."

"What's amazing about that?" Shaun said, casting out into a shadowy pool. "The crick's been closed to fishing all year."

Upon hearing this news, the big poacher dragged the little poacher into the car and fled back home, pursued all the way by phantom game wardens. I was so nervous I could barely still the shaking in my hands long enough to light my pipe. Even then I wasn't entirely successful, because a few seconds later it became apparent I was smoking part of my mustache.

At the time of the motorcycle ride invitation, Shaun, against all family expectations, had reached age eighteen.

"Don't be chicken, Unc," he challenged me. "Hop on behind. I want to show you how great it runs."

"Oh, all right," I said. Pipe clamped in my teeth, I climbed on. "Just up to the corner and back, okay?"

"Okay."

Roarrrrrrrrrrrrrrrrr! We went past the corner at Mach 2. The wind tore at my head. I clamped Shaun around the belly in a vicious bear hug, unable to risk turning loose long enough to reach his throat.

That is when the wind sucked the fiery dottle out of my pipe bowl and deposited it on the top of my head!

"How do you like it so far?" Shaun shouted.

"Stop, you fool," I shouted back. "My head's on fire!"

"Ho ho ho, what a joker! So you think this is fast, do you, Unc? Just wait until I take it out of low gear."

The wind presently removed the glowing dottle from my head, but not until it had burned a round, monkish hole down through my hair. The flaming chunk of tobacco couldn't have been on my head for more than a few seconds. But it seemed longer. Much longer. Time is relative, particularly when your head is on fire.

That and similar experiences added to Bun's store of reasons as to why I should give up my pipe. She once even accused me of thinking more of my pipe than of her.

"You'd rather sit up there in your office puffing away on that sop than talk to me," she snapped. "It's true, isn't it? Well? Well? Why don't you answer?"

"I'm *thinking*," I said. "No, after carefully weighing the pros and cons, I must say that I do prefer you over my pipe. No contest, really."

Even though my affection for Bun had come out ahead of that for my pipe, she was not satisfied. Apparently, she would have preferred that I skip over any thoughtful consideration of the matter and simply issue a snap judgment in her favor. Women have always been a puzzle to me.

As a consequence of this little marital misunderstanding, I boxed up all my pipes and locked them in a filing cabinet drawer, just to prove to Bun that I loved her more than them. That made her happy. The strange thing was, I scarcely missed the pipes. Sometimes I would go for minutes on end without even thinking of them. Every time I walked by the filing cabinet, I could hear the little devils calling out to me in their pitiful little pipey voices: "Pat, Pat, let us out! We'll be good. It's dark in here." But I would merely laugh and ignore their pleas. Quite frankly, I was amazed at my own willpower. Never before in my life had I displayed any strength of character whatsoever.

Then I went off to Georgia on a hunt with my old friend Charlie Elliott, a writer whose sterling prose has adorned the pages of magazines for half a century and more. Charlie, as might be expected of a Southern gentleman of his stature, smoked a pipe.

"Where's your pipe?" Charlie demanded.

"I gave it up," I said. "I'm working on improving my character."

Charlie claimed not to have any character to improve and went on happily smoking his pipe. One evening Charlie and I and some other fellows were sitting around the stove in a little turkey-woods cabin exchanging stories, some of them possibly true. Charlie got out his pipe and lit up, and then a couple of other fellows got out their pipes, and pretty soon the hunting cabin was filled with a fine cloud of smoldering pipe tobacco. It smelled of woods and turkeys and good stories and hunting and fishing and . . .

"Stop!" I cried, leaping to my feet. "I've got to find a pipe!"

"All right, calm down," one of the other hunters said. "We can find a pipe store in the morning."

"No!" I shouted. "Now!"

"Well, shucks," Charlie drawled. "I reckon we can find a decent corncob at that gas station we passed twenty miles up the road. Let's go get Pat a pipe. Won't take but an hour."

So we all piled into a car and drove to the gas station. The gas station man said he had sold all his corncobs, but there was a little store over in the next county that carried them. We drove to the store, Charlie and I ignoring cranky sounds emanating from the backseat. The store was closed. I could see a little card of corncob pipes through the window. So close but yet so far. Then Charlie remembered a little all-night shopping center a hundred or so miles into Alabama. He said he was sure I could find a pipe there. Upon hearing this, the other hunters burst into open rebellion, but Charlie fought them off and retained control of the car. He understood the serious need of a man caught in the grip of pipe denial.

We headed out of Georgia and into Alabama, despite much grousing and muttering from the backseat. At last, we found an all-night store in Alabama that sold pipes, and I bought one, a cheap little corncob apparently whittled into a pipe by an eight-year-old child with an excessive number of thumbs. It was, in short, quite wonderful. While our companions snored in the backseat, Charlie and I puffed contentedly away on our pipes as we cruised back toward Georgia. The sunrise, its golden rays glinting off the windshield, was beautiful. The whole morning was beautiful. Life was beautiful. Of course, it almost always is, when you're in the company of a good friend and your pipe.

It has been a long while now since I last smoked a pipe. Even that little Alabama pipe is locked away in a file drawer. Sometimes, late at night, hunched before a computer screen, I hear it calling me in its Alabama drawl. "Pat! Pat! Let me out! Let me out!" I hope Mr. Hacker addresses that problem in his next book.

Sam Spud and the Case of the Maltese Fly

(Once again the master sleuth triumphs over the forces of evil and an IQ of 38.)

Business had been slow at my detective agency—five years and not one client. I was beginning to think it was time to take up another line of work. Suddenly, everything changed.

It was one of those gray, dismal February mornings when tedium hangs in the air like smog. Or maybe it was smog hanging in the air like tedium. I got up and shut the window. Smog, all right. I didn't think it could be tedium, because my brassy receptionist, Flossie, and I had been killing a little time together, if you know what I mean. She was a former chorus girl and had legs that wouldn't quit.

"Would you quit with the legs!" I snapped at her. "I hate slow tap dancing. 'Tap . . . . . tap . . . . . tap . . . . . tap.' Cripes, Flossie, if you weren't eighty-seven years old, I'd think you were doing it just to annoy me."

"Age abuse! Age abuse!" she shouted. "Anyway, it takes you so long to make your play, I could do my whole tap routine between turns. A person who's spelling-disabled should kill time with something other than Scrabble."

While I was trying to think of a clever rejoinder, the door burst open. A panting, highly agitated gentleman stood there glancing about, a crazed look on his face.

"Something I can do for you, bud?" I asked.

"Excuse me!" he gasped. "I thought this was a men's rest room."

"It is," I said. "But the rent's what I can afford. There's another one down the hall you can use, if you don't mind a few rats and the occasional black widow spider." I forgot to mention the janitor's pet boa constrictor behind the toilet.

He rushed out and returned a few minutes later, obviously much relieved. Boa constrictors have their uses, I guess.

"Say, you're Sam Spud, aren't you?" he said. "I hear you're a dick."

"Some folks think so," I replied. "Actually, I prefer the term 'private eye.' What can I do for you?"

"First of all, my name is P. Elmo Figglesworth."

"I'm very sorry," I said, "but I can't help you there."

"It's not the name, you fool," he said pleasantly. "It's my wife. She's disappeared!"

"Aha!" I said.

"What do you mean, 'Aha!'?"

"Nothing. It's just a common private-eye expression. So, your wife has disappeared. I deduce you want me to find and return her to you. I get fifty bucks a day, and there's a small deposit for returns."

"No, no, I don't want her returned! If you'll just shut up for a moment, I'll explain."

Figglesworth then related a sordid tale so long and boring that Flossie and I went out for lunch in the middle of
it. When we returned, he was just getting to the summary.
As far as I could make out, he suspected his wife had
eloped with either the milkman or the postman, possibly
both. I deduced the milkman as the probable perp, because of the note Figglesworth had found. It was in his
wife's handwriting and said, "Two quarts of skim milk, a
pint of fat-free cottage cheese, and my bags are packed
and in the trunk of the car."

Fat-free cottage cheese! The woman was vicious. I
could see why Figglesworth didn't want her back. But here
was the kicker. His wife and the culprit had also made off
with the Maltese fly!

"The Maltese fly?"

"Yes," said Figglesworth. "As you probably know, it
was one of the last works of the great flytier Leonardo
Maltese. It's priceless. I'm willing to pay anything for its
return."

"Did I mention I get a thousand bucks a day and a
large deposit for returns?" I said. "Ah, I see you have pho-
tographs. Good. Let's have a look at them. So, this is the
milkman. Hmmm. Mustache, mean little eyes, muscular
build, obviously a dangerous character and . . . Pardon
me? Aha! It's not a photo of the milkman. In that case, I
deduce that the main object of interest for the milkman
was the Maltese fly, with your spouse coming in a distant
second and possibly only for heavy lifting."

Figglesworth concurred with my deduction. "There is,
however, the chance that the milkman has no idea about
the worth of the Maltese fly and merely scooped it up with
the rest of my fishing tackle. In that case, it's possible he
might actually try to fish with it and release the curse."

"The curse?"

"Yes! It's terrible. Anyone who actually fishes with the Maltese fly will instantly have all his skin fall off and, also, for the rest of his life will have very poor luck with dry flies."

"Interesting," I said. "I'll take the case. What's on my schedule, Flossie?"

"A dead fly and some dust."

"Luckily for you, Figglesworth, I've had some recent cancellations and am free to take up your case immediately."

Figglesworth gave me a photo of the Maltese fly and departed, absentmindedly forgetting about the return deposit, even as he managed to shake Flossie loose from his leg as he went out the door. I suppose Flossie thought I might use the deposit to pay her back salary, but I happened to know she was already knocking down $300 a month from Social Security.

The Maltese fly was spectacular in its plumage, no doubt at the expense of more than one endangered species. There would be no trouble recognizing it. I slipped into my detective garb and headed for the door.

"I see you're packin' a rod," Flossie said. "Looks a little light, if you ask me."

"It's a Loomis," I said. "A five-weight, two-piece graphite eight-footer. It can handle anything I run into, except possibly a steelhead over twenty pounds."

I stopped just outside the door and then stuck my head back in. "You're just jealous!" I said.

"What?"

That's one of the problems of playing Scrabble with Flossie. Every time I come up with a clever rejoinder, she's too obtuse to notice. The woman is slow.

Now my only problem was to find the milkman, one Rupert Holstein, and then separate him from the Maltese fly. As logic dictated, my first stop was the local dairy. A receptionist showed me into the office of the manager, Mr. Jack Hammer, a large and obviously irritable gentleman. "And you are . . . ?" he said.

"Spud's the name," I replied. "And danger's my game, excluding anything remotely life threatening. I'm looking for a Holstein."

"You've come to the right place," he said. "So what's your interest in a Holstein?"

"Fly-fishing," I said. "This Holstein is known to have engaged in fly-fishing in the past and—"

I thought I detected some disbelief on the part of Hammer, not merely because of his raised eyebrows but also because he had picked me up and was about to hurl me like a javelin into the parking lot.

"Do I take it, then, Mr. Hammer, that you have no knowledge of a Rupert Holstein?" I responded calmly to the top of his head.

"Oh, *Rupert* Holstein!" he exclaimed. "Yes, we do have a Rupert Holstein. Sorry about the misunderstanding, old chap. But Rupert just turned in his resignation and is at this very moment clearing out his locker."

Hammer used me as a pointer to direct my attention out the window to the parking lot. "That's his car, the black-and-white one painted to resemble a Holstein cow."

Five minutes later I was slouched down in my own car, watching for my quarry to come out. His car wouldn't be too difficult to follow in heavy traffic, because I had detected a large, distinguishing crack in the rear window. On the other hand, it was getting dark. So I had resorted to an old private-eye trick for tailing a vehicle at night.

Holstein suddenly emerged from the dairy, got into his vehicle, and disappeared into the darkness. "Aha!" I mused to myself. "Apparently, you're not supposed to break *both* taillights."

Before dawn next morning I had Holstein's house un-der close surveillance. He stuck his head out the door, glanced around to make sure the coast was clear, and pay-ing no notice of the snowman that had mysteriously ap-peared in his yard overnight, went back in and soon returned, attired in his fishing duds and carrying a fly rod. He got in his car and drove off.

It wasn't my lucky day—perhaps not all that surprising, since my last lucky day was in 1953. By the time I could shed my disguise and thaw myself out, Holstein was long gone. But he had by no means outfoxed me.

The only fly-fishing water clear of ice was the Blight River. I immediately sped to the best fishing hole on the Blight. Sure enough, there he was, precisely as I had sus-pected. I could just barely make out his car parked on the far side of a pasture near the river. Then all at once the car moved off into a wooded area. Perhaps he had spotted me, but if he thought he could shake me off his tail that easily, he was badly mistaken. Half an hour later I pulled into a farmer's barnyard. But enough about that.

Thinking Holstein had finally given me the slip, I de-cided there was only one thing left to do. I returned to the river, unpacked my fly rod, and was about to cast when I noticed another fisherman standing no more than a dozen feet from me on the other side of some brush. "Holstein!" I shouted as I leaped over the brush and stayed his arm in midcast, for there, tied to his tippet, was none other than the Maltese fly!

"Stop!" I cried. "You're about to release a curse!"

"You're right about that," he grunted as we writhed about on the bank. And then he released one. It was pretty bad, too, although nothing compared with The Curse of the Maltese Fly.

I finally managed to wrest the rod from his hands and

send him whimpering on his way. It felt good. I had actually solved my first case. But just then I noticed a nice rainbow hanging behind a rock ten feet from shore, well within my range. Without thinking, I cast to it.

The Curse of the Maltese Fly really hasn't bothered me excessively, probably because I never had much luck getting dates, anyway. I do miss fishing with dry flies, though.

Other Than That,
Bostich . . .

Mr. Bostich Crane, Associate Editor
Pretentious Men's Magazine
New York City, New York

Dear Bostich:

I imagine by now you are back in your New York office working hard on your article about me for your series in *PMM*, "Real Men in the Outdoors." I know it will be a dandy. I can't tell you how flattered I was to be selected as one of your subjects for an article.

We are all fine here. Retch Sweeney and the other boys down at Kelly's Bar & Grill told me to say "Hi!" so I will—"Hi!" They enjoyed your visit every bit as much as I did, particularly those who had the opportunity to partic-ipate in our little adventure. Allow me to make a suggestion, however. I don't think it would be a good idea to use up a lot of space in your article writing about the boys, although it wouldn't hurt to mention them briefly. In my many years of writing, I have found it is best to focus almost exclusively on your main character, which in this case happens to be old me. Ha ha!

Much to my delight, you got to experience Kelly's on a Saturday night. I was hoping you'd get to watch the Saturday Night Fights, but everybody was on his best behavior because you were there. The boys wanted to create a good impression, with the exception of Luke, who had imbibed a little too much and tried to do his striptease act. Fortunately, Kelly was able to hit him with a pool cue before the act got too offensive.

I did get a kick out of Kelly's asking you what you wanted to drink.

You: "Martini?"

Kelly: "Nope, my name's Kelly. Now what wouldja like to drink?"

It's a good thing you didn't ask for a Bloody Mary. She's one of the waitresses. You would have been in a whole heap of trouble, man.

Thank you very much for the classy new suit of outdoor clothes. I had forgotten that *PMM* devotes a great many pages to fashion and fashion advertising. For many years, Henry P. Grogan, owner and proprietor of Grogan's War Surplus, who is not likely to advertise in *PMM,* has been the fashion designer I have most relied upon for what we in Idaho consider the proper outdoor look, or Idaho Chic, as this style is often referred to. The nice thing about it, we feel, is that it is equally appropriate for casual social occasions or for gutting an elk, not that I have gutted all that many elk, ha ha. This is by no means meant to disparage the fine set of outdoor duds you bought me, no indeed. I look very classy in them and am often asked if I am on my way to the opera, even though there isn't an opera within five hundred miles. But it's nice to be asked anyway. I think the photos of me in my spiffy new clothes will fit right in with those of the gaunt, sensitive young men who model your fashions, the only difference being that I am somewhat less gaunt and sensitive, ha ha. But I guess you know that.

Personally, I thought the camping trip we "real men" went on was one of the more enjoyable that I've had lately. I trust you are not too concerned about the photographer you brought along to shoot the pictures. He appeared to be a fit young man, and I am sure he will turn up one of these days.

How's the old tailbone? Still sitting on the rubber donut, ha ha? The boys, by the way, scored that fall of yours an eight on the usual scale of ten. They did not deduct any points for the scream, but they felt obligated to take off a point for your failure to come up with a humorous remark after you regained consciousness. The humorous-comment requirement applies all the way up to a number ten fall, where it is omitted for obvious reasons. I mention this only so that you will be more cognizant about the scoring of falls on your next outing with us, which I trust will be soon.

I hope you are not under the impression that I knocked you off that log over the ravine. Even though you might have supposed that I had lost my balance and lunged at you, the fact is I was trying to grab you and hold you on the log. Regretfully, despite the initial contact, I was too late. That I stepped on your fingers during the few seconds you clung to the log merely hastened the inevitable. In a situation like that, it is best to get it over with as quickly as possible, as I'm sure you will agree.

Well, at least you got to see the method for constructing a litter out of a couple of poles and some ponchos out in the wilds. Practice makes perfect, as they say. The litter worked rather well, if I may be so immodest as to mention. Of course, there is always the problem that while crossing a rain-swollen stream over slippery rocks, the litter bearers will lose their footing and drop the litter. And wouldn't you know there would have to be a big rock right under your injured tailbone? Isn't that just the way? Man, I bet you scared all the local wildlife into the next state.

Thank goodness we were able to catch up with you and the litter right after you went through the rapids and before you went over the falls. The falls would have been a ten, no doubt about it. It's really quite pointless trying to think up a humorous comment on your way over the falls, even though you'd have plenty of time to do so. Ha ha.

In the future, though, I think we will avoid tying the injured party to the litter while crossing a river. That way he might make more profitable use of his limited time scrambling to safety rather than frantically trying to untie a bunch of knots underwater.

It's too bad we couldn't get you out of the mountains that day, but I'm sure you enjoyed that extra night of camping out. After a hard day of tramping through the mountains, there's nothing like a good hearty meal of fried bacon, fried potatoes, fried beans, fried bread, and fried coffee. Only joking about the coffee! Seriously, I can't explain the grease in the coffee, but I'm reasonably sure it was just plain lard, not boot grease or anything like that. All the guys got a big kick out of your joke: "Anybody bring Rolaids?" That was a good one. We still repeat it from time to time, and practically laugh ourselves sick. You are one comical guy, Bostich!

Looking back I can now see that it was a bad idea to allow Retch Sweeney to make S'Mores for dessert. S'Mores. That's the concoction for which Retch roasted marshmallows over the fire, placed them over pieces of chocolate bar, and sandwiched the whole mess between two graham crackers. S'Mores are Retch's culinary specialty. It's an old Girl Scout recipe. Girl Scouts love S'Mores but two or more are fatal to adults, which is why we didn't offer you a second helping, not that you asked for one. No, they aren't fried, ha ha.

Now, in regard to the flaming marshmallow, the best I have been able to ascertain about that is Retch slapped at a mosquito on the back of his neck, and in so doing flicked the flaming marshmallow onto your sleeping bag. Because the sleeping bag was sopping wet, the marshmallow should have been immediately extinguished, but, as you know, it landed on the one dry spot. You might think some of these old sleeping bags are insulated with some combination of gunpowder and dry leaves, the way they burn once ignited. That is the reason Retch didn't hesitate to stomp out the flames. Usually, the person in the sleeping bag is physically capable of ejecting himself from a flaming bag, but, of course, in this instance, that wasn't the case for you, since we had the sleeping bag tied to the litter in an effort to stabilize your tailbone. Looking on the bright side of the stomping, you already have two kids. Did you enjoy the songs around the campfire?

The last day of the trip was rather boring, as I recall. Oh, yes, there was that incident with the grizzly we ran into on the trail. If I'm not mistaken, you looked a little perturbed when we dropped your litter—littering, we call it, ha ha—and took to the trees. Once again, grizzlies are another good reason for not tying the injured party to the litter. Even with two broken legs, a fellow can still manage to go up a tree like a squirrel at the sight of a grizzly headed his way. Motivation is everything, as I'm sure you know, given the fact that you managed to stand up and run a few feet with the litter strapped to your back before, alas, toppling over.

Nevertheless, I'm sure also that you are aware that it is impossible to climb a tree while holding a litter, and that you won't think the less of us in that regard. As you may have noticed, even though your eyes were squeezed tight shut, as were ours for the most part, because grizzlies can do some really nauseating things to people, stuff you really don't want to watch, well, as I say, you may have noticed that the grizz was more curious than anything, and all he did was sniff you all over before wandering off.

All the experts recommend holding your breath while being sniffed by a bear, and you did that remarkably well, just as if you had an instinct for what to do and required no instruction on the proper procedure. But after the bear leaves, you are supposed to start breathing again, and that is where you slipped up. While we were drawing straws to see who would give you mouth-to-mouth resuscitation, you finally started breathing on your own, and let me tell you, Bostich, that was a big relief to all of us, particularly me. And the fact that I'd drawn the short straw had nothing to do with it. I mean that sincerely.

Fortunately, after we finally made it out of the mountains, Doc Mean could find nothing he regards as a serious injury, although I must report that while he was wiggling your tailbone about to see if it was broken, you cleared that waiting room of patients. Son, you could make a fortune as a healer. The ill and the lame were instantly cured and abandoned crutches, canes, and even wheelchairs as they raced one another for the exit. It was all I could do not to flee myself.

After we loaded you and your rubber donut on the airplane, we stood around and waited for the takeoff, partly because we don't have much entertainment in our lives but mostly because we wanted to see you on your way. You must not have noticed all of us waving, because you didn't wave back. But perhaps the neck brace and the bandages on your fingers prevented you from doing so. Now, in regard to that article you're writing about your little adventure with me, Bostich, I think it would be well if you held the flattery to a minimum. A little would be fine, of course, but try not to overdo it. As I said at the beginning of this letter, I know your article will be a dandy.

Please come back and see us at first opportunity. We've got a chair reserved for you down at Kelly's, and we're always ready to hit the mountain trails at a moment's notice. But it wouldn't hurt to call first.

Oh, I just this minute heard that your photographer chap turned up. But enough about that.

Looking forward to our next adventure together, your old Idaho friend,

Pat

The Chicken-Fried Club

I checked my watch. It was almost time. The phone rang. I answered it. A woman's voice said, "March Brown, this is Evening Pale Blue Dun." The voice was sexy and warm, taut with anticipation of a shared and illicit passion. I hung up.

"Who was that?" my wife asked.

"Wrong number," I said.

"I'm about ready to start supper," she said. "We're having sauce of tofu with brussels sprouts over lentils."

"One of my favorites," I said, "but I've decided to fast this evening. Occasional fasting seems to give me increased energy and alertness."

"Good," she said. "I didn't want to cook anyway. I think I'll sit down with a nice bowl of raw carrots and watch some exercise programs on TV."

"Don't tempt me," I said. "Maybe I'll just take a little five-mile walk."

I put on my trench coat and Scottish wool shooting hat. I pulled the hat brim down low over my eyes.

"Very dashing," she said. "Nobody would ever recognize you in that getup."

That was the idea. I would have worn my fake mustache, but I already had a mustache. Two mustaches are a dead giveaway.

There were spies everywhere. Informants lurked even among friends and relatives—particularly among relatives. If they detected your slightest deviation from the norm, it was instantly reported. You had to be careful, very careful. Times had changed.

I walked down the street, listening for the sound of footsteps behind me. I turned and pretended to be studying some of the bodybuilding machines arranged in the window of Joe's Body Shop. I could remember when body shops took the dents and bulges out of cars. Now, they took them out of people. I checked my rear. Well, too late for that. Good reason to wear a trench coat. I then checked the street. Nobody in sight, except for a solitary jogger. He loped on by, his legs pink and pebbly. Either he was wearing a pigskin bodysuit or he had been out in the cold too long.

Just past Verleen's Health Spa, I paused for a moment at Edna's Health Foods and glanced back. The coast was clear. I picked up my pace and turned into an alley, stepping over a derelict sprawled asleep on the concrete, an empty bottle of cheap carrot juice clutched in his grimy hand. I shook my head in disgust. Something had truly gone wrong with our society.

At the end of the alley I knocked three times on the red door. A gruff voice said, "Password?"

"Emerging Caddis," I said.

The door opened. A beefy man stood there. He grabbed me by the lapel of my trench coat and pulled me up close to him. I could feel his eyes moving over the features of my face. Not a good feeling, a little too moist for my taste, and the eyelashes tickled. One of the worst cases of myopia I had ever encountered. The halitosis wasn't that great either.

"Okay," he said. "You can go on up."

At the top of the stairs, I came to another door. It was guarded by a mug wearing a long black coat, but the coat didn't conceal the bulge under his right arm. From the size of the bulge, I guessed an automatic, probably a 12-gauge with full choke, no plugs. This guy meant business. He gave a little toss of his head, indicating for me to go in. I opened the door.

The room was crowded with people from all walks of life, stockbrokers, carpenters, beauticians, hotel maids still in uniform, matrons with diamonds cascading from beneath their chins and dripping from plump earlobes. The room fell silent. The looks turned on me bristled with suspicion and, perhaps, even fear.

"He's okay," a woman said. "He's one of us."

I recognized the sultry voice of Evening Pale Blue Dun. She approached from across the room, weaving her way among the crowded tables, the occupants of which were once again engaged in a din of conversation. Evening Pale Blue Dun wore a shimmering blue dress that looked as if it had been painted on, one coat, no primer.

"Glad you could make it," she said, her voice reminding me of a smoldering campfire that would burst into flame from the slightest puff of air. Her eyes turned hard for a brief instant.

"Do you always blow in people's faces?" she said.

"Sorry," I said. "It's an old camping habit."

"You bring the goods?"

"Yeah."

"Let's have it."

I handed her a sheet of paper.

She stared at it. "What's this? 'Cleaners, haircut, return books to library . . .' "

"Sorry. Wrong paper."

I dug another sheet from my pocket and handed it to her. Her face contorted in wild ecstacy as she scanned the paper. "Yes! This is it! Yes! Yes! Yes!"

I almost expected the earth to move. It didn't. Then, suddenly, her lovely hazel eyes became icy slits of suspicion.

"Are you sure this is authentic?" she demanded, thrusting the paper under my nose.

"I'm sure. It's Zumbo's secret recipe. I took notes while he was preparing it in a Wyoming hunting camp."

"Does he know you have it?"

"No. And he'd better not find out, either."

She clutched the paper to her ample bosom. "Oh, this is so wonderful! Jim Zumbo's own secret recipe for chicken-fried elk steak!"

She took me by the arm and led me to the table. "This little offering buys you membership in the Chicken-Fried Club."

"Thanks," I said. "I figured it would."

As I pulled out a chair and joined a couple of other diners, the lady bent over and whispered huskily in my ear. "But where can I find an elk?"

"That's your problem, Evening Pale Blue Dun," I said, and it wasn't all that easy to say, either. Even if I'd known where to find an elk, I certainly wouldn't have told her.

The occupants at the table introduced themselves: Wooly Worm and Hare's Ear, their code names, I assumed.

"March Brown," I said, shaking hands.

They went back to their plump, juicy, golden chicken-fried steaks. "The waiter will bring yours in a minute," Hare's Ear said. "There's no limit, either. Eat all you want."

"The hash browns look delicious," I said. "They have that nice sparkling sheen of hot grease, so essential to true hash browns."

"I see you're a true connoisseur of fat," Wooly Worm said. "By the way, old man, sorry for the cold reception you got when you first came in. We thought for a moment you might be with the Fat Police. You can't be too careful these days."

"I know," I said. "They're everywhere."

Just then a waiter came around with a huge serving tray stacked high with steaming chicken-fried steaks. I took only a couple, in order to leave room for a substantial load of mashed potatoes and gravy. The coffee was dark and rich, fairly sizzling with caffeine. I dribbled thick cream into it.

"I can't begin to tell you how delighted I was when Evening Pale Blue Dun invited me to join the Chicken-Fried Club," I said.

"You were most fortunate," Wooly Worm said. "We'd just had a sudden opening among the membership." He and Hare's Ear bowed their heads.

"Yes, poor Black Gnat," Wooly Worm said. "He was sitting right there in your chair, matter of fact. Suddenly just flopped over, his face in his mashed potatoes."

"Good heavens," I said. "Sounds like a cardi—"

My companions spewed food all over the table. Almost ruined my appetite.

"Never speak that word in this room!" Wooly Worm hissed. "You'd be ejected immediately! And rather forcefully, you can be quite sure!"

"Sorry," I said, glancing about. "I only meant to say 'cardigan,' the sweater, you know. Cardigans can be quite deadly."

Wooly Worm and Hare's Ear regained their composure. "Yes, quite right, old man," Wooly Worm said. "Cardigans must be avoided."

As I was leaving, Evening Pale Blue Dun came up and took me by the arm once again.

"That was a very nice gift," she said. "I hoped you enjoyed yourself."

"It was terrific," I said. "By the way, since you're the one who runs this club, I was wondering if by any chance you're into fly-fishing?"

"Hardly," she said. "Why do you ask?"

"No reason."

"Be back next week?"

"Sure. After all, this is the last place in the country where you can get chicken-fried steak."

She turned those warm, inviting eyes on me. "Anything special I can do for you next time, big boy?"

I thought for a moment.

"Yeah, there is," I said.

"What's that?"

"Biscuits and gravy."

She smiled and winked.

I opened the door, paused for just a second, then looked back at that shimmering vision that was Evening Pale Blue Dun.

"*Sausage* gravy."

Into the Twilight,
Endlessly Grousing

The Old Man was sitting across from me at the kitchen table in his cabin, polluting the air to lethal levels with a large illegal cigar someone had smuggled in to him and that his doctor had ordered him to stop smoking anyway.

"I know Doc ordered you to give up those cigars," I said. "Your smoking them is bad for my health."

"That's because you're a pantywaist," he said. "This is a fine cigar, and if you had any taste at all, you'd appreciate its lovely aroma. Hemingway always brought me a couple boxes from Cuba when he came up to hunt with me in Idaho. Now, there was a man! They don't make men like Hem anymore, yourself being a case in point."

"I've heard all your Hemingway stories and don't believe a one of them," I said. "But they've improved over the years."

"Practice makes perfect," he said. "I ever tell you the time I outshot Hem on a grouse hunt? He wouldn't speak to me for two days afterwards, he was so mad. So then I let him beat me in arm wrestling, and then he was okay. I loved grouse hunting best of all. Almost best of all. Say, I got an idea. Let's go grouse hunting."

"You're too old and almost blind," I said, kindly. "You can't see more than ten feet ahead of your nose. How are you going to shoot grouse?"

"You leave that to me," he said. "Now don't just stand there with your mouth hangin' open. Get me down one of my shotguns. The French twelve-gauge side-by-side will do."

"You gave that gun away years ago," I said.

"Well, that was a durn fool thing for me to do. Who'd I give it to?"

"Me."

"You! I would never give you a shotgun. You must have stole it."

"Nope, you gave it to me. It's mine now, and I'm keeping it. Anyway, it's much too fine a shotgun for a dirty old man like yourself. It's a gentleman hunter's gun. It's surprising any decent gun dealer would sell a fine instrument like that to an unsavory character such as yourself."

"Interesting you should say that," he said. "I tried to be a gentleman hunter once, but it didn't take. Belonged to one of them elegant shooting clubs. Had to dress up like we was going to an afternoon tea rather than on a hunt. They had all these pheasants penned up like a bunch of chickens, and whenever we got ready for a hunt, one of the hired hands let a hundred or so of them loose and we'd go out and shoot them. The pheasants was tame, of course, so we'd practically have to kick them up in the air in order to get them to fly. So one day I says to the president of the club, I says, 'Howard, this is a big nuisance, hunting pheasants this way. Why don't we just shoot them in the pens and be done with it? Save both the pheasants and us a lot of bother.' Well, that made Howard and some of the other gentlemen mad, and they booted me out of the club. So I quit the club right then and there. Figured it would teach them a good lesson."

"Served them right," I said.

"I thought so. Now, stop standin' around jawing at me. If we're gonna go grouse hunting, we got to get to it. Fetch me the little Brit twenty-gauge."

I went to find the 20-gauge. It was as fine a gun as I'd ever seen. The Old Man had been rich once, his guns now the only evidence of that former wealth. I figured he'd become rich by accident or inheritance, because as far as I knew he'd never worked. He was not the sort of man who would waste much effort on becoming rich. It had been a long time since he'd outlived his wealth, along with all his friends and enemies. "Mostly I did it to spite my enemies," he'd say, "but it got my friends, too."

He was very old now, ninety at least, maybe even a hundred; it was hard to tell, because he lied about everything, particularly his age. He was one of those peculiar old men who somehow managed to spend their entire lives enjoying themselves. He'd done just about everything there is to do, and what he hadn't done, he simply lied and claimed to have done that, too. He was a very irritating old man, and I couldn't understand why I put up with him. I handed him the gun.

"Good," the Old Man said. "I was worried that you might have stole this one, too."

"Just an oversight," I said. "I'll come back and get it some night when you're asleep."

"Ha!" he said. "That will take some doing. I ain't slept

in twenty years. Now, here's my idea. We'll go out to that good grouse woods behind Jake Gregory's farm, and you can flush some birds toward me, and I'll snap shoot them as they pass through my field of vision."

"Can't," I said. "Jake Gregory's woods is now a golf course."

"A golf course! They turned a good grouse woods into a golf course? I hate golfs! Well, we can go out there anyway, and you can flush some golfs toward me. How about that?"

"I don't think so."

"I know. We can go out to the mountain where Rance Crabtree used to live and—"

"A shopping mall."

"A shopping mall! Good gosh a-mighty, what's a shopping mall doing way out in the country?"

"It's not way out in the country anymore. It's in town."

"They moved the mountain into town?"

"No. They moved the town out to the mountain. They've got condos all over the mountain."

"Condos? They good to eat?"

"Kind of tough and not much flavor. Taste a lot like golfs."

"Hunh. I don't like shootin' stuff ain't fit to eat. Unless, of course, it gets to be a nuisance. Let that be a lesson to you. Ain't there any good grouse woods about no more?"

"I know a couple spots. But I like to keep them a secret. I show them to you, you'll be sneaking out there and shooting all my grouse."

"You bet. Now stop your yapping at me and let's go."

"Oh all right," I said. "While you're walking out to the car I'm going to have only another cup of coffee or two and maybe read the newspaper. So you'd better get started."

"I've been started for the past five minutes. Shows how observant you are!"

I drove the Old Man over to my house and managed to kill a little time there while my wife, Bun, babied him and fed him sponge cake with huckleberry sauce and whipped cream. She doesn't permit me to have whipped cream, a good indication of how much she prefers the Old Man over me.

I got my own gun and a vest full of shells, and considered whether to take the dog's shock collar. The collar works wonders for instilling obedience, but I wasn't sure how it would affect his pacemaker.

I finally extracted the Old Man from the fawning attention of Bun and inserted him back into the car.

"That's a fine woman," he said, licking remnants of whipped cream from his mustache. "She married?"

"You know she is," I said. "To me."

"You! What a waste!"

I drove out to one of my secret grouse woods and put the Old Man on a stand well out of range of my car. He sat down on a stump with the gun across his lap and a dead cigar clamped between his teeth.

"This is a good grouse woods," he said. "It's a little blurry but it smells right. You're too ornery to find me a nice clear grouse woods, but at least you found one that smells right. It sounds okay, too."

"Good," I said. "I'm going to circle around through the woods and see if I can flush some grouse toward you. Don't shoot anybody."

"I'm glad you mentioned that. Otherwise, I wouldn't have known. If a golf comes by, I might try for it, though. How much lead on a golf?"

"A couple of feet if it's driving a cart flat out. If it's walking or running, you can pretty much hold right on. But there's a big fine if you shoot one."

I strolled off through the woods, enjoying it, absorbing it, feeling the press of birch leaves under my boots, listening to the rustle of small wild lives dart unseen for cover, smelling all the pungent smells of a grouse woods in late fall. I shot my first grouse in this same woods when I was about twelve, an amazing shot that would have been even more amazing if the grouse had been flying, instead of sitting on a limb. I was hunting all alone, the hand-me-down 12-gauge shotgun big as a howitzer, and both barrels had gone off simultaneously and knocked me flat on my back, skinned up my trigger finger, and bloodied my nose. I thought the gun had exploded, and was glad still to be alive, but it had shot true and killed the grouse stone dead. My mother was enormously pleased with the grouse, marveling that her son had brought home wild game, and she cooked it in a gravy to pour over rice, and that one grouse could have fed twenty people, with some left over for the dog. I forgot to mention to anyone that the grouse had been sitting on a limb, but a kid can't be expected to remember everything.

I walked all the way through the woods and came out near a road on the other side, and by then I had three grouse, enough for my mother to have fed an army. All three shots were amazing, all wing shots, too, with the grouse *burrrr*ing off through the trees, but none so amazing as the shot that took that first grouse fifty years ago. Did I say *fifty*? Surely I meant twenty. Yes, it couldn't possibly have been more than twenty years ago.

"How'd you do?" the Old Man asked me. "I heard a dozen shots. Even you must have got something with a dozen shots."

"Three grouse," I said. "How about you?"

"I did fine," he said. "None for none. It was a good hunt. This is a great grouse woods. By the way, what does that sign say over there? I been thinking about walking over so I could read it, but then I figured I might not make it back before dark."

"That sign. Oh, it just says, 'Private Property. No Hunting.' "

"Is that all?" the Old Man said. "I thought it might be something important."

On the way back to town, the Old Man mentioned that he'd got hungry from all his exertion. "Let's stop and get a bite at Gert's Gas 'N' Grub."

"You want to *eat* at Gert's Gas 'N' Grub?" I said. "Why, you must be half starved, and crazy besides!"

Gert herself came out to visit with us, and all the waitresses gathered around and made a big fuss over the Old Man, and he ate it all up, along with a chicken-fried steak and hash browns with gravy poured over them. He joked with the waitress and tried to pinch Gert on the behind, but she was too quick for him, as was almost everyone. Then a couple of the local boys joined in the festivities, and after a while one of them asked what we'd been up to.

"Grouse hunting," the Old Man said.

"Get any?" Red Barnes asked.

"I only got three," the Old Man said. "The boy here, he didn't get none. Did a lot of shooting, though, so he had some fun. It was a good hunt."

"Well, I guess your eyes are still plenty sharp then," Gert said.

"Yep," the Old Man said. "Mighty sharp for a man my age—thirty-nine and some. Well, we best be going. Pay the bill, boy, and leave the girls a big tip."

We didn't get back to the Old Man's cabin until after dark, and he was pretty well tuckered out, although still smiling over all the attention heaped on him by the girls at Gert's. "I guess I still got it," he said.

"Yeah, right," I said. "It's just that you've got so old the women know you're harmless. First you get harmless, then you get lovable. That's the way it works with women."

"You're just jealous," he said.

I helped him to his cabin and was about to close the door behind him when I suddenly remembered. "Wait a minute," I said. "You left your gun in the car. I'll go get it."

"Naw," he said. "Keep it. Save us both the trouble of you stealing it from me later. That was a fine grouse woods. Mighty fine. I'd thank you for taking me there, but it'd just give you a big head."

I drove on home, happy in a way about the gift of the gun, but also not so happy. When you get right down to it, a gun is only a gun. I was glad it had been a good hunt, though, and I was even more glad that I had lied about the sign next to the grouse woods. What it actually said was, "Future Site of the New Grouse Haven Golf Course and Condos!"

Dream Fish

The great fish came to me in a dream.

I was ten years old and fishing was practically my whole life, all else mostly filler. At the moment, I was trapped, perhaps terminally, in fourth grade. The only thing that could save my sanity was Opening Day of Trout Season, and it lay far off in the future, somewhere beyond eternity. And then came the dream. It went like this:

It is spring, Opening Day of Trout Season, and I'm down on the creek in the eerie light just before dawn. I see the fishing hole as clearly as if I'm actually there, it's all so real. The weather has been cold, must have been cold, because the melt-off in the mountains hasn't come yet. Otherwise, the creek would be running high on Opening Day of Trout Season—up near the top of the banks, the water the color of a chocolate shake, and about as thick. But in the dream, the creek flows low and clear.

I am familiar with this particular hole, have fished it often in real time. The creek divides around a little willow-clad island at this spot, a narrow stream going down one side of the island and the main stream down the other. The main stream ripples across a gravel bed, then deepens into the hole, a dark placid pool beneath an overhanging stump at the end of the island.

A log crosses the small stream, a convenience supplied by the dream to keep me from getting my feet wet in the icy water as I cross over to the island. The dense willows on the island prevent me from approaching closer to the hole, just as it does in ordinary life, but a tiny protruding gravel beach provides me a place to stand for a straight shot at the hole, a drift of about fifty feet. I prefer fishing a much shorter line, and although I don't think so at the time, it seems to me now that the dream, which had been rather accommodating so far, would have provided me with a little closer access.

I remove the sinkers from my leader so as to get the necessary drift without hanging up, and then send the worm on its mission. This is no ordinary worm, but one chosen for its strength, courage, and intelligence, the Sir Lancelot of Worms. I feed the line bit by bit from my level-wind reel, which no longer level-winds, because in an earlier and frightening part of the dream, I have taken the reel apart and cleaned it. Not likely! But this, of course, is only a dream, and one does foolish things in dreams, like cleaning a reel the week before Opening Day of Trout Season.

Through my dream's omniscient vision, I see the great fish lurking in dark depths beneath the stump, surrounded by bare, hook-hungry roots, the roots apparently supplied by the dream for the purpose of suspense. Peeking over the Cabinet Mountains, the sun suddenly rolls a shower of diamonds flashing across the creek, and at that very moment the great fish glides out from among the roots and sucks in the worm. The rod twitches ever so slightly. I heave back, arms straight and quivering above my head. Beads of water fly sparkling from the line as it snaps taut in the air, and I feel for the first time in my life the surging power of a truly big fish, a fish that will not surrender to the indignity of being flipped ignominiously back over my head and plopped on the bank, my standard method of landing fish.

The straining leader cuts a slow arc in the surface of the pool, the fish not giving an inch, taking its time, contemplating its next move. The submerged roots are dangerously close. I haul back hard on the line, but I can't hold the fish away from those gnarled and grasping tentacles an evil tree had sent down into the earth a century ago for the sole purpose of depriving me of the great fish.

And then, as if the beckoning roots aren't bad enough, the worst possible thing happens. Mrs. Smithers, our fourth-grade teacher, rudely awakens me with some stupid question about the capital of North Carolina! Just as if that were something I might be expected to know! What could she have been thinking of? As Mrs. Smithers taps angrily on a map with her pointer, the great fish swims into oblivion, about halfway between Greensboro and Winston-Salem.

Later, I tried to pick up the dream where it left off, to see how it turned out, but I never could.

Around the end of May each year, cutthroat would come up the creek to spawn, and that would be my one chance to catch really big fish. The water, typically, would be swift and murky and high up on the banks, and for about a week I could catch cutthroat up to maybe eighteen inches, and sometimes did. But then the water would recede, the cutthroat with it, and the resident brookies and I would be left to contend with one another over the summer.

That was the problem with the dream fish. Because of its size, I was almost certain it had to be a spawning cutthroat. But that particular hole couldn't be fished on Opening Day, when the cutthroat were running, because the water was always too high for me to reach the island, the willows too thick to permit access from the far bank. But it had been only a dream. A dream can do anything that suits its fancy.

I made the mistake of telling Retch Sweeney about my dream fish.

"So?" he said. "What's your point?"

"Nothing," I said. "But don't you think it's interesting?"

"No."

"Well, I guess you had to be there."

"Don't put me in your dreams, I'd die of boredom. You want dreams, I'll tell you dreams. Make your hair stand on end!"

"But don't you see, Retch? Maybe the dream was trying to tell me something."

"Like what?"

"It could be trying to tell me to fish that hole on Opening Day."

"It could be trying to drown you, too. Ain't no way you can get near that hole on opening day."

I had a little better luck telling my dream to the old woodsman Rancid Crabtree.

"Now, thet is interestin'," he said, biting off a chaw of tobacco. "Ah'm purty good at interpretin' dreams. Maw momma taught me how to do it. You see, a dream never comes at you straight on. Nothin' in a dream is what it seems to be but always somethin' else. And once you figger out what the somethin' else is, then you gots to go along with it."

"Really, Rance? Can you tell what my dream means?"

"Jist hold yer hosses, boy, it's startin to come to me.

Now, the way thet fish pole of yourn was choppin' up and down, Ah suspect it was really an ax. Yep, thet's it, an ax. Now, thet big stump, it's got to mean wood of some kind—firewood! Gots to be firewood. And the big strong handsome fish, thet gots to be me."

"But what does it mean?"

"It means you should go out thar in the yard and chop me up a big pile of firewood. Ain't no doubt about it."

I preferred to interpret the dream for myself. It was less work. I knew what it meant, anyway. It meant that I was supposed to fish that hole on Opening Day, no matter what.

The rest of the school year crawled by with ever-diminishing momentum. I began to fear that it would stop entirely and I would be trapped forever in fourth grade, a fear not without basis. But with a sudden burst of energy in the final weeks of school, I learned the capitals of all forty-eight states, conquered long division, learned to multiply and divide fractions, and memorized the Gettysburg Address. Contrary to all my expectations, school finally ended for the year, and I was promoted to fifth grade with what Mrs. Smithers described as a "photo finish," whatever that meant. And now a whole endless summer of fishing stretched before me. It was, after all, a perfect world.

Shortly after the passing of eternity, Opening Day of Trout Season Eve finally arrived. I went to bed at eight, my plan requiring me to be on the creek no later than five. I set the alarm clock for four-thirty. But the clock was a treacherous and evil thing. It could be depended upon to awaken me for school without fail, but it had no regard for fishing. It couldn't care less if I went fishing or not. I lay awake worrying about the treachery of the clock.

Then it occurred to me that I may have talked too much about my dream fish. It would be just like Rancid or

Retch to beat me to the hole, in the off chance my dream had correctly prophesied that the great fish would be there. Why had I been so stupid to tell them the dream! Yes, it was quite possible and even probable that they would try to beat me down to the hole and claim it for themselves. I reset the alarm for three-thirty. Still, that only gave me a margin of thirty minutes to secure the hole by four. Why take the chance? I reset the alarm for three. That would be cutting it close. Even then the alarm might not go off. I continued to lie awake worrying about the evil clock. Midnight came and went. One o'clock ticked by. Two o'clock. I was still wide awake. Well, better safe than sorry. I got up and went fishing.

The weather had been unseasonably cold all during May, and the melt-off hadn't come yet. The creek would still be running low and clear, just as the dream had predicted. So far, so good. I shivered as I walked through the starry night, not because of the cold or my ancient fear of the dark, but out of sheer anticipation. The grass was tall and wet, and soon my pants were soaked and dragging on me, my tennis shoes had gone all icy-squishy, and mosquitoes came up out of the grass like fierce squadrons of Luftwaffe. It was wonderful. This, after all, was Opening Day of Trout Season. What more could a kid ask for?

For two hours, I hunkered on the high bank above the creek, waiting for the first hint of dawn, shivering so violently a passing observer would have seen only a blur. Gradually, reluctantly, night began to lose its grip on the valley. It was almost time. As the sun began its climb up the far side of the Cabinet Mountains, I slid down the steep bank to the creek. Ahhh! There was the island, the creek forking around it, but the log promised in the dream as a bridge to the island was missing. Was it possible, if the dream had deceived me about the log, that it had also deceived me about the great fish? I waded through the icy water. Pain shot up my legs, which soon grew numb and comfortable, numbness serving as a kid's insulated waders in those days. The gravel beach was there, still above water, offering me a straight shot at the hole. My hands were so cold I could barely hold the squirming Sir Lancelot. The hook finally baited, I set it adrift toward the hole beneath the stump. Had the great fish been only a malicious trick played upon me by the dream? A tiny doubt began to tug at me. But then, even as I had begun to question the dream, it happened, a strike so wild and powerful and savage it was almost terrifying!

As I see it now in slow motion, perhaps even as I saw it then, the great fish came straight up out of the water, bursting into that bright spring morning of the Opening Day of Trout Season. Huge and magnificent and real at last, it rose high above the surface of the creek and then, slowly, slowly, majestically, rolled into a one-and-a-half gainer, all the while violently shaking its massive head. Then, still in slow motion—oh, the horror, the *horror* of it!—the fish broke free!

I have since forgotten much bigger fish, fish I actually caught, but I have never forgotten the dream fish that, for one brief instant, became gloriously real. It survives today as brightly in my mind as it did when I was ten years old. So perhaps in a way I did catch the dream fish, inducting it as I have into the mythical legions of The Ones That Got Away, those fish that live on as long as memory lasts. And so, you might ask, do I not deep down believe it was a far, far better thing for the great fish to have slipped once more beneath the dancing diamonds of Sand Creek and to have darted away into the watery depths, still wild and free? Fat chance.

Will

It had been a good hunt but had gone on way too long. It was time to quit.

"You can't quit now," Jack said. "Give it a couple more days."

We were more or less bivouacked in a big old abandoned ranch house equipped with shutters that pounded incessantly in the wind. Camping inside a drum would have been quieter. I still count Jack and his brother Ben, both scarcely out of their teens, among the best guides I've ever had. They were in the kitchen, busily assembling the day's sack lunches for their clients, the rest of whom were finishing breakfast in the dining room.

I walked back into the dining room and poured myself another cup of coffee.

Marcella said, "If Pat leaves, I'm going with him. I can't

stand another *bleep*ing day of this *bleep*ing wind! It never *bleep*ing stops!"

"If it stops," I said, "half the ranchers in Montana fall over."

Marcella was blond, pretty, and had mastered the pout. Her pout had been kind of cute at first, but cute has its limits. Marcella's pout had now gone way beyond cute and was pushing the envelope of serious irritation. She was possibly married to Bennett, but in any case they had come on the hunt together. Bennett, who seemed to have grown oblivious to Marcella's existence, was one of those fiercely macho hunters who make guides regret they dropped out of college. But I will say this for him. He had a really nice haircut.

The other couple at the table, Will and Jane, were in their eighties. Will was terminally ill, and his doctor had warned him that if he came on this hunt, he'd die. Will replied that if he didn't come, he'd die. So he and Jane had flown out from Chicago in their private jet. If my wife and I make it into the eighties, I hope we are just like Will and Jane—filthy rich! I jest slightly.

Will and Jane were fine and elegant and brave and smart, and they had hunted all over the world together for just about everything it's possible to hunt. Jane got a nice antelope on the first day of the hunt, but Will had had no luck at all, without much time left now—for anything— and every day seemed to take a greater toll on him. Because he was hunting, he refused to take his painkillers, but he remained chipper and funny and classy, and I knew this would turn out to be a truly rotten hunt if Will didn't get his pronghorn. I feared that if that happened, Ben, the old man's guide, might go off and do something truly awful to himself, like become a lawyer.

I groaned loudly for Jack's benefit as I hoisted my legs one more time into the battered Suburban.

"What's wrong now?" Jack said.

"Just extreme pain," I said.

"Don't worry. You'll loosen up."

"That's what you always say."

Marcella and Bennett were in the backseat, Marcella slouching in a pout in one corner, Bennett looking intense. I hate for an armed person to sit behind me when he looks that intense. Bennett had his hunt for the day all mapped out, and he directed Jack to drop him and Marcella off at the top of a ridge. He strode off through the sagebrush with Marcella pouting along behind, rifle slung over her shoulder. We watched until they disappeared down a wash.

"I wonder if Bennett has ever read Hemingway's 'The Short Happy Life of Francis Macomber'?" I mused aloud to Jack. "You know, where you think Macomber's wife is going to shoot a Cape buffalo but instead she shoots—"

"You would have to mention that," Jack said. His forehead wrinkled into a worried frown.

It wasn't as though in the past five days we hadn't seen some antelope that were more than satisfactory, as far as I was concerned. Disgusting as it is to admit, I was thinking of antelope more in terms of chops and sausage than size of horns.

"Look, Jack, there's a nice buck," I'd say. "It'll do fine."

"Naw. I want to get you a really good one." That's the problem with good guides. They won't settle for less than the best.

I was a bit puzzled as to why I'd come on this hunt anyway. I wasn't in my hunting mode. I'd driven all the way from my home to eastern Montana, figuring that my hunting mode would kick in on the way. It hadn't. Still, the hunt had been good, because just being in Montana is good, but I was tired and stiff and sore and old, and I knew it was time to quit.

The Suburban slid to a stop in a cloud of dust. Jack

grabbed the glasses and scoped some brown-and-white dots in the far distance. Cripes, I thought, I hope those brown-and-white dots turn out to be just brown-and-white dots.

"There he is!" Jack said. He handed me the binoculars. Sure enough, there he was, a truly magnificent pronghorn standing aloofly off from the herd, an arrogant fellow too proud to mix with lesser of his kind.

"Great," I said. "The only problem is we'll never get close enough for a shot. There's no cover for us within half a mile of him."

"Sure there is," Jack said. "See, we can crawl down that dry creek bed to the flat, and then we can crawl on our bellies to that little rise to the left of him. That'll get us within four hundred yards of him, at least."

"So?" I said. "As I mentioned before, we can't get close enough for a shot."

An hour later we were crawling on our bellies through the sagebrush. If you haven't hunted antelope in Montana, I should mention that the way you crawl on your belly through sagebrush with a rifle is with the rifle slung around your neck and swaying under your chin. In this way the sling cuts off most communication between your body and your brain, so your brain doesn't realize that your body is in extreme discomfort, until, of course, the time comes to remove the sling from your neck. Then your body yells, *"Pain!"* Eastern Montana, by the way, happens to be the sticker capital of the world, which you realize only if you crawl on your belly through a sizable portion of it. Every year Montana exports huge quantities of stickers imbedded in the hides of out-of-state hunters who have crawled on their bellies in quest of an antelope.

"How you doing?" Jack whispered.

"Yowp," I replied.

"Good, we're almost to the rise."

"Yowp."

"We're getting pretty close. So stop the whining."

"I'm not whining. Don't you know a death rattle when you hear it?"

Twenty minutes later I slid up alongside Jack, who was peering over the rise. "He's still there," he said.

I unslung the rifle from my neck—*"Pain!"* my body screamed; *"major pain down here!"*—and then set the crosshairs to dancing about in the general vicinity of the pronghorn. Through sheer willpower, I steadied the rifle and fired. Dust flew up no more than ten feet behind my target. Pretty fair shooting if you ask me, but Jack didn't ask.

Antelope can reach a top speed of sixty-one miles an hour, slightly less than the speed limit for cars at that time. In approximately two minutes, the herd had raced across the valley floor, up and over a mountain, and disappeared into the valley beyond. And here I had forgotten to bring my baseball bat. When your guide has spent hours getting you into position for a shot and you miss, you instantly whip out your bat and hit the guide over the head with it, but only as a safety precaution.

Jack seemed stunned anyway. He was still staring at the place where the antelope had once stood.

"I guess that's it," he said.

"Yeah," I said. "It's time to quit." I didn't mention that the antelope had looked much too tough for steaks and chops.

That evening, as we neared the pickup spot for Marcella and Bennett, the headlights illuminated Marcella walking down the road. Alone. She turned and began hopping up and down and waving her arms. There was no sign of Bennett.

"Good grief!" Jack said. "I was afraid of this."

"Looks bad," I said. "She isn't pouting."

We pulled up alongside her. "I shot him!" she cried.

Jack rested his forehead on the steering wheel. "Dead?"

"Yes, dead! Hit him right in the neck!"

I tried to comfort Jack. "At least he didn't suffer."

"Bennett's dragging him up to the road right now," Marcella added. "Boy, is he ever ticked! He missed and I didn't!"

"Ah, an antelope!" Jack said.

As we drove back to camp, Marcella related every last tiny detail of how Bennett had missed and she hadn't. Bennett took our ribbing better than I expected, although I can't say I care much for pouting in a man.

When we got to the ranch house, Ben was just walking back toward the empty Suburban after helping Jane and Will into the house. He stopped and stared glumly at us. We stared back, equally glum. Suddenly, Ben's face erupted into a huge grin, and he wiped imaginary sweat from his forehead and flung it on the ground. With a dramatic flourish he jerked open the rear doors of the Suburban, and there was Will's antelope! It didn't look like a trophy by any means, but it was by far the most wonderful pronghorn I'd ever laid eyes on. Even Jack said he'd never come across a better one, and he'd seen one heck of a lot of antelope.

Through the living room window, we watched the old couple toasting each other, no doubt with some of Will's fifty-year-old Scotch.

"See," Jack said. "You don't ever want to quit till it's over."

"Yeah," I said. "I guess the trick is knowing when it's over."

Leaning into the wind, I limped off in the direction of Will's fifty-year-old Scotch.

Crime Wave

The world is going to the criminals, no doubt about it. I know, because right here in our little town of Blight, Idaho, we've recently had a crime wave. It's scary. Some folks even started removing their keys from the ignition when they park their cars. I've also heard about a couple of elderly ladies who took to locking their doors at night. It's bad.

I first learned about the crime wave from Delmar Foot. Delmar was obviously pleased to be the one to break the news to me. We don't have much news here in Blight, so the opportunity to pass it on is something to be relished. Makes you feel kind of like Dan Rather on the *CBS Evening News*.

"You heard about old Henry Sly, Pat?" Delmar asked.

"Nothing good," I said. "What's he done now?"

"You ain't heard, then?"

"No, I ain't."

"It's about Sly's chain saw. A deputy sheriff come out and investigated."

After presenting this teaser so I'd stay tuned for the news, Delmar took the Blight version of a commercial break. He dug out his can of chew and stood there thoughtfully studying the lid, as if he couldn't remember the combination. I expected him to say, "I'll be back with the chain saw story, right after this."

"Skip the teaser, Delmar," I told him. "What about the chain saw?"

"It got stole."

"It got stole?"

"Yep. Right out of old Sly's garage. Somebody walked in and snatched it, pretty as you please."

I was shocked, much to Delmar's satisfaction.

"Yep, stole it right out of his garage," Delmar said, recapping the news.

"What did the deputy do?"

"Nothin'. He just looked in the garage and said, 'You're right, ain't no chain saw in here. Guess it got stole.' Didn't dust for fingerprints or talk to nobody what might've been an eyewitness to the crime or check for tracks or nothin'. Can't tell but what the deputy might have turned up some of that DNA stuff if he'd investigated a little more careful."

"Clearly a breakdown in law enforcement," I said. "Chain saws are practically loaded with DNA."

"Darn tootin'! Now, here's the peculiar thing." Delmar took the lid off his snuff can and loaded up his lower lip.

I was getting a little irritated with Delmar's teasers. "So, what's the peculiar thing?"

"Well, it's just this. Old Sly had a brand-new five-horse

outboard motor settin' right there in plain sight in his garage, and the thief didn't take that. He took an old wore-out chain saw instead."

"If I was a thief, I'd have taken the motor," I said.

"Me, too!" said Delmar. "Ain't no heavier than a chain saw—and a lot more fun!"

"You're right about that," I said. "From my vast experience with criminals, I know they'd rather steal things that are fun rather than things that are work. Back when I was in college, I actually shared an apartment for a while with a professional thief, and his specialty was sporting goods."

"Wow! That's weird!"

"Yes, indeed, he was a real criminal and—"

"No, I mean—you went to college?"

"Yes, Delmar, I did. I hope it doesn't show."

"Don't worry, Pat, it don't."

"Good. Anyway, about my roommate . . ."

I had moved out of the university dorm and into a small hovel off campus. The dorm had gotten much too rowdy, with horseplay going on all hours of the night and endless practical jokes being played on serious students trying to get an education. The dorm supervisor narrowed down the problem to two instigators of the mischief, as is often the case, and to solve the problem, suggested that Duke and I find an apartment off campus. Well, we were both relieved, because it had become almost impossible for us to get any studying done with all that ruckus going on.

I didn't know much about Duke, except that he could short-sheet a bed in thirty seconds flat. And he was terrified of snakes, even the harmless garden variety. The mere mention of snakes would cause him to shudder. He would even check his shoes each morning to make sure a snake wasn't curled up in one, as if snakes commonly hung out in a college dorm. Other than that bit of absurdity, he seemed okay, although something less than a serious student like myself.

"What's in that box?" he asked suspiciously as we were moving into the hovel.

"Books," I said.

"Oh," he said. "I thought it might be a snake."

"Geez, Duke," I said. "You've got to get over this abnormal fear of snakes. Besides, if it will make you feel any better, I sold the snake to Artie Feldman. Artie said he could put it to good use."

For the first few weeks, Duke and I got along fine, even though he had quite a few irritating habits and wasn't all that keen on personal hygiene. But he had a car and I didn't, and a roommate with a car can be excused quite a few shortcomings. Duke was several years older than I, even though we were both freshmen. I wasn't sure whether he had been in the service or had just lingered a few years longer than normal in high school. I suspected the latter.

Shortly after our move into the hovel, Duke disappeared for a couple of days. Upon his return, he asked me to help unload his car. The trunk was full of golf clubs and tennis rackets.

"Holy cow!" I said. "Where did you get all the clubs and rackets?"

"My uncle died and left them to me."

"How come he needed so many rackets?"

"Just liked to have some spares on hand."

"Boy, I guess. He didn't even remove the price tags."

"Yeah. You want a racket? I'll sell you one cheap."

"Naw. I don't tennis."

About once a month, another of Duke's beloved uncles would die and leave him a bunch of brand-new sporting equipment, which Duke would store in our hovel. After a while, we could hardly see the walls, there was so much stuff piled against them. I suggested to Duke that members of his family were dropping off with abnormal frequency.

"Yeah," he said. "It's real sad. Wanna buy a bowling ball?"

Then one day Duke showed up with a whole carload of rifles, shotguns, binoculars, fishing rods, and reels. This was more like it.

"Another uncle die?" I asked.

"Yep. Dear old Uncle Fudd. I'll really miss him. This here was his favorite shotgun."

"I can see that. He kept it in the box it came in."

"That's right. Uncle Fred always said, you own a fine firearm, you got to take care of it."

"Fudd," I said.

"Who?"

"You first said your uncle's name was Fudd. Now you just referred to him as Fred."

"Right. Fred Fudd. You wanna buy the shotgun? Since we're such good pals, I'll sell it to you real cheap."

"Sorry. No money."

I would dearly have loved to pick up a few of the guns real cheap, as well as some of the fine rods and reels. My heart ached with envy just looking at them, or at least at the boxes that contained them. My sporting needs would have been filled for life. On the other hand, not being entirely stupid—forget the unfounded rumors spread by my professors—I had belatedly arrived at the conclusion that my roomy was a professional thief. We had so much hot merchandise in our hovel, the heating bill dropped to practically nothing.

Still, I was reluctant to confront Duke about the matter. He was surly, large, and muscular, and I was mild, thin, and puny, about the right size, in fact, to fit nicely into the trunk of a car, even when rolled up in a carpet. I could have called the cops, but I had no proof that Duke's sporting uncles hadn't had a sudden run on their mortality. On the other hand, I was expecting a police raid on our hovel at any moment. Surely they would suspect me as being an accessory to the crime. So there was nothing for me to do but bring the matter to a head with Duke, and sternly so, regardless of the consequences to myself. I only hoped I wasn't being too harsh.

"Say, listen, Duke, ole buddy. I got an idea. You have plenty of money, so why don't you move to a nicer and larger apartment and take your loo—uh, your stuff, with you?"

"Naw. I like it here. Besides, when I'm off going to funerals and like that, I got you here to keep an eye on my loo—uh, my stuff. Nope, I'm staying right here, ole buddy."

What to do, what to do? There seemed no way out. Sooner or later Duke was bound to get busted, and I right along with him:

"You see, Officer, he said his nine uncles recently died and left him all this stuff, and I believed him. I had no way of knowing I was harboring a criminal and his loot."

"Sounds reasonable to me, son. Cuff him."

I began to see there was only one way out of the fix. I had to get rid of Duke. It was a terrible thing to contemplate, but there was nothing else to do. I'd just wait till Duke was asleep some night and . . . First, though, I had to arrange a rendezvous with a shady character of my acquaintance.

"You bring it?" I asked, glancing around the darkened alley to make sure we weren't under surveillance.

"Yeah. You bring the dough?"

"Yeah. Let's see the merchandise. Okay, looks good, this should do the job."

"Worked for me. I got rid of my roommate with it."

"It's untraceable, too," I said.

"Sure. There are millions out there exactly like it, all unregistered."

"You got that right, Artie."

A day later, Duke was gone. The only damage was to the hovel walls, where Duke had ricocheted about trying to get a clean shot at the door. He later came back and collected his loot. And none too soon either. The police raided his new pad a couple of weeks later, and I never saw or heard from him again.

And now, more about our crime wave in Blight. Delmar rushed over to tell me the latest.

"Got some more news on Sly's chain saw," he said. Then he took out his knife and began cleaning the dried mud from his boot cleats, this being his first opportunity to do so since buying the boots.

"Get on with it, Delmar," I said.

"Oh, all right. Well, whoever stole the chain saw brought it back. Put it right in Sly's garage."

"Now, that's really interesting. From my vast knowledge of psychology, Delmar, I can tell you that the thief probably felt guilty and realized how stupid it is to sneak around in the night stealing folks' tools."

"I suppose. But then I guess he had second thoughts."

"How so?"

"This time he took Sly's motor."

So the crime wave in Blight continues.

Attack of the Stamp People

If it hadn't been for Lester Osgood, I would have been just another happy-go-lucky fourth-grader without a care in the world, except possibly for long division. Instead, I had to worry constantly about being nabbed by the evil Stamp People. Hard telling what the Stamp People might do to me, but it wouldn't be anything pleasant, I was sure of that.

I lived on a little farm and Lester lived in town. One day after school, he invited me home with him. I was surprised to discover he lived in a fine house surrounded by huge trees and a lawn the size of our cow pasture. His bedroom was filled with games and toys of all kinds, including an electric train so wonderful it could eat your heart out from pure envy. For the first time I realized that Lester was rich. But was he happy? You bet!

"Wow!" I said. "Let's play with your train, Lester."

"It's kind of boring," he said. "It just goes around and around on the tracks. What I want to show you is my stamp collection."

Stamp collection? Why would Lester want to collect stamps, unless, of course, he wrote a lot of letters and didn't want to be caught short of postage?

Lester took a large album from his bookcase and opened it on the bed. I was amazed. It contained beautiful stamps from all over the world: big stamps, little stamps, square stamps, oblong stamps, and even triangular stamps. Lester flipped through the pages, pointing out stamps from Brazil and Africa and India and New Zealand, just about anyplace I could imagine and even places I couldn't imagine.

"This is wonderful!" I cried. "Gee, Lester, you're so lucky to be rich enough to collect stamps!"

"Oh, you don't have to be rich to collect stamps," he said. "It helps, of course, but it doesn't cost much at all to get started. Here, I'll give you one of my old beginner stamp albums."

I opened the album and stared down at all the little spaces practically crying out to be filled with stamps. "Gee, thanks, Lester," I said. "But I better not take the album. I don't have any money to buy stamps."

"Sure you do," Lester said, thereby revealing he hadn't a clue as to the meaning of the word "poor." He opened a copy of his *Magazine for Boys*. "See this advertisement? 'Send only twenty-five cents to the Stamp People for a packet of two hundred assorted stamps!' Surely you have a quarter, Patrick."

"Oh, sure, I have a quarter," I said, chuckling. I didn't mention the quarter was about half of my life's savings.

Lester tore out the page with the stamp advertisement

on it and gave it to me. "You can't go wrong on two hundred stamps for twenty-five cents," he said.

Lester was pretty smart about most things but, boy, was he ever dumb about that!

The very next day I sent off my quarter to the Stamp People. Several weeks went by with no response, and I was beginning to think the Stamp People had stolen my quarter. Then one day a bulky little packet arrived. My fingers trembling with excitement, I tore it open and dumped the stamps out on our kitchen table. Ahhh! My stamp collection had begun! The stamps weren't nearly so beautiful as Lester's, and many were duplicates of the same stamp. But there were a few nice ones, too, and even a few from foreign countries. "Neato!" I said to myself.

I found it strangely satisfying to paste my stamps into the album. Afterward, though, I felt mildly depressed. My stamp collection had both started and stopped with the twenty-five-cent packet.

Scarcely a week later another packet of stamps arrived from the Stamp People. There were no duplicates this time, and all of the stamps were practically new. Obviously, the Stamp People had got to thinking that maybe they should have sent me a better grade of stamps in the first place. Now they were trying to make up for their error. I tossed the empty packet and the few papers it contained into the wastebasket and happily began pasting the stamps in my album.

Soon another packet of really terrific stamps arrived! And then another! And another! My bedroom was practically aflutter with stamps. Frantically, I pasted stamp after stamp into my album, rushing to keep up before still more packets arrived. But after a while, I began to get this uneasy feeling. Why did the Stamp People keep sending me stamps? Maybe I had misread the ad. Maybe it had said,

"Send us a quarter and we will send you stamps forever!"
Or maybe the Stamp People were simply kind and extremely generous folks, wishing nothing more than to help
a boy get started on a wholesome and educational hobby
like stamp collecting. It finally occurred to me that the papers I'd discarded with the latest packet might contain
some explanation of the Stamp People's generosity, but, as
bad luck would have it, Mom had already emptied the
wastebasket. I did vaguely recall some fine print on one of
the papers.

Then the packets stopped coming. I was disappointed,
of course, but I really couldn't hold that against the Stamp
People. They had certainly given me more than my quarter's worth of fine stamps.

One day when I returned home from school, Mom
said, "Guess what, you got a letter. It's from those Stamp
People."

I was pleased. Not only had the nice Stamp People sent
me more stamps than I had ordered, they were now writing to me. Probably they were asking if I was satisfied with
all my free stamps. I took the letter to my bedroom and
opened it.

"Dear Patrick," the letter began. "As one of our most
valued customers, we hope you have been happy with the
stamps you have received from us." Valued customer!
That was nice. "However," the letter went on, "it has apparently slipped your mind that you now owe $12.50 for
additional packets of fine stamps. We would appreciate
payment as soon as possible. Thank you for your immedi-
ate attention to this matter. Sincerely yours, The Stamp
People."

Twelve dollars and fifty cents! If it had been a million
dollars, I couldn't have been more shocked. Nor would it
have made any difference. I doubted my whole family

could scrape together $12.50. So, the Stamp People weren't so kind and generous after all. From the tone of their letter, on the other hand, they did not seem unpleasant or unkind, which was good, because there was nothing for me to do but ignore them. I hid the letter under my mattress.

Pretty soon another letter arrived from the Stamp People, this one much less friendly. It went something like this: "Pay up right now or else!" Nervously, I tore up the letter and threw it away. "Or else" what? Why hadn't they been more specific? Were they thinking of calling in the police? "Patrick, we know you are in there! Your house is surrounded! Come out with your hands up! Bring the stamps!"

Next letter: "We have ways of dealing with deadbeats! Pay up! We know where you live, Patrick. Don't make us come get you!"

I cornered Lester at school and told him about the letters from the Stamp People.

"No problem," he said. "Just send back their stamps."

"I can't! I pasted them in my stamp album!"

"You *pasted* them in? You shouldn't have! There are special little sticky tabs you're supposed to use so the stamps can be removed without damaging them."

Sticky tabs? So now he tells me!

"How would it be if I sent them my album with the stamps pasted in, Lester?"

"I don't think they'd like it."

A lot of help Lester was. He'd lured me into a life of crime and then had no idea how to get me out of it.

I couldn't sleep. I couldn't eat. I checked my hair every morning in the mirror to see if it was turning white from worry.

"What on earth is wrong with you?" Mom said at dinner one evening. "You hardly touch your food anymore."

"Nothing," I said.

"Really?" she said. "Then why is it I see you peeking out through the curtains of the front windows all the time? Are you expecting someone?"

"No," I said. It was a lie. I was expecting the dreaded Stamp People.

I thought maybe I should go into hiding. But where? Under my bed? That would surely arouse my mother's suspicion that her son the criminal was on the lam. Besides, under a bed was probably the first place the Stamp People looked for people who owed them money. I wondered if maybe a disguise wouldn't be better. On the other hand, a fourth-grader in a mustache and dark glasses might only call attention to himself.

As I was peeking out through the curtains one day, a dark van pulled up and stopped in front of our place. Two men got out. One of them carried a large net with a long handle on it, perfect for dragging a kid out from under a bed!

"It's the Stamp People!" I yelled at my mother. "They've come for me! Don't open the door!"

"Hush!" Mom said, opening the door. "It's only the dog catchers. I reported that stray dog that's been running around biting people."

After she had told the dog catchers where they might find the mean dog, Mom turned her attention on me. "Now, what's this about stamp people coming for you?"

There was nothing to do but confess my crime.

"Why on earth did you order stamps you don't have money to pay for?" Mom yelled. She was not taking this well. I began to sense I might be better off in the hands of the Stamp People.

"I didn't order them! They just came and I pasted them in my album, so I can't return them! I thought they were free! And now the Stamp People are out to get me!"

"You didn't order the stamps?" Mom said. "They just came? And now the Stamp People have the nerve to threaten my son? In that case, I'll handle this."

She then sat down and wrote the Stamp People a letter. I never heard from them again. They may have been tough, but they were no match for an angry mother. As for me, I found another hobby. My nerves just weren't up to the high-stress world of stamp collecting.

Big Ben

I had just settled into a chair on the patio and was unwrapping a cigar when I glanced up and saw Eldon advancing across the backyard. Eldon is the annoying little rich kid who lives next door. He had obviously managed to climb over the board fence that separates our two yards.

"Eldon," I yelled at him. "Why do you think I cemented broken glass to the top of that fence?"

"To keep out burglars. Well, it won't work. I just toss a folded blanket on the glass and climb on over. Burglars could do the same thing. They're not dumb, you know."

"Is that right? Well, maybe I'll have to install coils of razor wire along the top of the fence. Now go home. I'm busy."

"How can you be busy? You don't have a job."

"I do have a job. I write. At this very moment, I'm busy writing, or at least I would be, if a little boy wasn't yakking at me. What do you want, anyway?"

"I was just wondering if you had any sand I could use for my dump truck."

"No, I don't have any sand for your dump truck. What does this look like, a beach? Oh, I suppose you could take some out of the little box over there on the back porch. The box next to the cat's dish."

"Thanks."

"You're welcome."

"Since you're being so nice to me, Pat, you can come over to our yard and watch me do sparklers on the Fourth of July if you want."

"Watch you do sparklers? Well, that's some excitement to look forward to."

"Yes, it is quite exciting. Did you get to do sparklers on the Fourth when you were a boy?"

When I was a boy, on the Fourth, my friends and I *were* sparklers. If a kid was caught smoking, it was probably because he had just stopped flaming. The Fourth wasn't considered a success unless you ended up looking like an elongated cinder.

I was well into my teens before I realized the Fourth wasn't a season but only a single day. What kind of Fourth is that, one measly day? No, our Fourth stretched from the middle of June, when the fireworks stands opened up, until the entire supply of fireworks in the county was exhausted. And fireworks were really fireworks back then. Some of the rockets could have stopped tanks. There were firecrackers big enough to blast out stumps. The people who sold the fireworks, however, were very careful about selling dangerous fireworks to just any kid who happened to stop by. They had safety standards. A kid had to be old enough to pronounce the word "fireworks." After he'd passed the security check, he'd say, "Now gimme two anti-tank rockets and a flamethrower."

Even if you ran out of money for fireworks, you could stand in your yard at night and watch flaming projectiles shoot up into the air from around the neighborhood. "Oooo," you'd say. "That was a nice one!" Or, "Ahhhh! I liked that one best. What was it?"

"I'm not sure, but I think it was the Mahoney kid."

I didn't mention any of this to Eldon, but I myself was rather timid around fireworks. It was my older cousin Buck who tried to teach me how to throw firecrackers.

"See, it's easy," Buck said. "Here's how you do it. One, grasp firecracker between your fingers. Two, light the cracker. Three, cock your arm. Four, throw the cracker." Buck threw the firecracker. "See, it's easy. Just go through the steps, one through four, in a nice smooth motion."

"Great, Buck! I'll try it." I went through the steps. One . . . two *BANG!*

"People who aren't that good at counting shouldn't throw firecrackers," Buck said.

"I can't feel my hand!" I yelled. "I can't feel my hand!"

"Don't be such a sissy. Your hand's fine, unless, of course, you might want to use it sometime."

My hand didn't look fine, although some of the little blackened twigs bore a slight resemblance to fingers.

Mom was sympathetic. "That'll teach you to throw firecrackers. Now go back outside and stand under the sprinkler. How many times do I have to tell you, no smoking in the house!"

Eldon came back with his little bucket full of sand. "If you didn't do sparklers on the Fourth, what did you do?"

"Well, actually, Eldon, our Fourth was pretty quiet when I was a kid." And it was, too. Most of the guys took the day off to recover from their injuries. There was the parade through town to watch, and the picnic afterwards. My stepfather, Hank, and I had a tradition of getting up early the morning of the Fourth to go fishing. We never caught any fish, but Hank said he just enjoyed getting away to the mountains and having a wilderness experience.

One Fourth of July fishing trip, we stopped to eat our lunch on a gravel beach. Hank had a really fine fishing outfit, including the first pair of chest waders in our part of the country. I still had a few firecrackers left, and while we were eating our sandwiches and Hank was enjoying the tranquillity of the moment, I decided to set a few of them off, just to break up the monotonous tranquillity.

"I wish you'd stop that," Hank said. "I hate firecrackers. You're ruining my wilderness experience!"

"I only have one left," I said. "Look at this baby, Hank."

"Holy cow! What is that ugly thing?"

"This fat little devil here is what's called your Big Ben! Cost me a whole dollar. Now, get ready, because I'm gonna light it and toss it."

"You sure it's your last one? I really hate this." Hank put his hands over his ears and turned his head away.

I'd lied. I actually had two Big Bens! Hank loved a good practical joke, and he couldn't help but get a big kick out of this one. My timing had to be perfect. "Get ready, Hank. I'm lighting it now." I held both firecrackers in one hand, lit one, dropped it, and tossed the unlit one down the front of Hank's chest waders.

"Sorry, Hank!" I said. "The wind blew the Big Ben down your waders."

There was no wind, but a person doesn't pay a lot of attention to meteorological conditions when he has a Big Ben down the front of his waders.

Hank yelled out a really bad word and frantically tried to shake the Big Ben down one leg of the waders, his objective clearly one of damage control. If a game warden had come by, he might have arrested Hank for obscene dancing on a trout stream. Then the firecracker on the ground went off. *KaBOOOOM!*

Hank shot straight up in the air. His sudden and significant gain in altitude startled me. For a second, I wondered if maybe I had tossed the wrong firecracker down Hank's waders, but, no, there was the smoldering debris on the rocks.

"I can't feel anything!" Hank shouted. "I can't feel anything!"

It took me a while to explain the practical joke to Hank, but eventually he got a big laugh out of it. About five years later, as I recall.

The only damage to Hank was emotional, mostly psychosomatic, and that faded after a few days. When we got home, Hank still wasn't speaking to me, and before he stomped off to his den, all he said to my mother was, "Firecrackers! Firecrackers! I hate firecrackers!"

"Well!" Mom said. "Why's he acting so strange?"

"Oh, you know Hank," I said. "He always gets a little grumpy when we don't catch many fish."

"No, I mean why is he walking so funny and talking in that high, piping voice?"

Eldon set his pail of sand on the table and made himself comfortable in a chair.

"Don't bother making yourself comfortable, Eldon," I said. "I told you, I've got work to do."

"Okay. I just wanted to know if you're going to come over and watch me do sparklers on the Fourth. It's pretty scary."

"I'm sure it is. And I definitely will be over to see you

do sparklers, unless, of course, I have an extremely contagious disease at the time and am running a high fever."
Cough cough.

"Great! Well, I'd better get this sand back over to my dump truck."

"Good. By the way, Eldon, don't worry about the little lumps in the sand. You can crumple them up with your fingers."

Roast Beef

My family was so poor that when the Great Depression came along, it was an improvement. "Let the good times roll!" my mother shouted.

Some of our neighbors were even worse off than we were. One whole summer my friend Ronnie Figg didn't have shoes to wear. He didn't mind, because he thought going barefoot would exempt him from church. But then Mrs. Figg, who was much more religious than Ronnie, came up with a solution. Before church on Sunday, she had Mr. Figg paint a nice pair of black oxfords on Ronnie's feet. They looked really elegant, too, unless it rained. The paint job, of course, had to be renewed every Sunday, and the oxfords never turned out quite the same. As a result, it appeared to the congregation at their church that Ronnie had a whole closet full of new shoes, and there was some talk around the church about the Figg family putting on airs. So Mrs. Figg told her husband to paint a regular old pair of tennis shoes on Ronnie's feet and let it go at that. As any artist would be, Mr. Figg was disappointed, because he had spent a great deal of time mastering wing tips.

I don't know if all that's true, about the painted-on shoes. It's just what Ronnie told me one day years later, when we were comparing our childhood hardships. Still, I can't imagine Ronnie would lie about something like that.

After my father died, it sometimes seemed as if we ate nothing but gruel. My mother was a great believer in "Let's pretend." She had a theory that ugly reality could be improved upon by a mere act of imagination.

"Tonight, let's pretend the gruel is roast beef!" she'd exclaim cheerfully. "Oh, this is excellent 'roast beef,' children. Now, don't just sit there staring at your 'roast beef.' Eat your 'roast beef.' Didn't you hear me? I said, *eat your roast beef!*"

"How come we always have to have 'roast beef'?" I'd complain. "Why can't we ever have 'hot dogs'?"

"Oh, we can, we can. Tomorrow night we'll have 'hot dogs,' just for you, Patrick. And 'chocolate sundaes' for dessert! Yum! Doesn't that sound good?"

One evening while my sister, Troll, and I waited for Mom to bring a steaming bowl of gruel out from the kitchen, I called out hopefully, "What's for supper, Mom?"

"Venison steaks and pancakes!" she called back cheerfully. "Doesn't that sound good? Yum!"

Troll shot me a look that said, "Give me a break!"

Then Mom bustled out of the kitchen, carrying in one hand a big platter of pancakes and in the other a platter of venison steaks!

"It *is* venison steaks!" Troll yelped. "Where did you get those, Mom?"

"Someone left them on the back porch last night. They were all wrapped up in a newspaper."

"I wonder why he sneaked them onto the porch in the middle of night," I said. "Why didn't he just give them to us?"

"Well, it's not exactly deer season, you know," Mom replied. "Some kind soul is just trying to help us out in hard times."

"I don't think he's so kind if he poaches deer," Troll said.

"There's still leftover 'roast beef,' " Mom said.

"Pass the venison, please."

Every so often, our secret benefactor would strike again. Always the venison was left wrapped up in newspaper on our back porch in the dark of night. Neighbors reported receiving the same nocturnal gifts. The mystery of the secret benefactor's identity was almost as delicious as the venison he distributed. Still, there was the knowledge that we had a poacher among us, and poachers were held in contempt by our law-abiding, game-warden-fearing neighbors. So it was generally thought best to allow the mystery to remain a mystery.

Although no one wanted actually to say it, there was some suspicion that the poacher might be the odorous old woodsman Rancid Crabtree. It was well known that Rancid lived pretty much off the land, his aversion to work possibly even surpassing his aversion to water. Still, it was hard to imagine Rancid stooping so low as to poach deer.

One night Ronnie Figg and I decided to sleep out in the woods behind his house. I wasn't too keen on sleeping out, but Ronnie was depressed because his dog, Sparky, had been missing for several days. I thought sleeping out with him might cheer Ronnie up. It was one of my first sleepouts away from home, however, and I was a little worried that it might be too scary, overload my circuitry and short it out, with the result that I would flee camp in the middle of the night. News of a guy's fleeing camp in the middle of the night usually spread like wildfire around the neighborhood, where it would be remembered for the next forty years and worked into conversations at every opportunity:

"Boy, the nights are starting to get warm, aren't they, Mr. Jones?"

"Yes, indeed they are, Patrick. Very much like that night forty years ago when you fled home from that sleep-out. Ha!"

It was the kind of embarrassment one did not want attached to one's reputation for the rest of one's life.

Fortunately, the sleep-out with Ronnie was great fun, and I wasn't the least bit nervous, even though Ronnie and I were exchanging some really hideous ghost stories. Much to my relief, I learned that I was a lot braver than I thought. Quite possibly I possessed nerves of steel, as I had long suspected.

Then it got dark.

The ghost stories tapered off rather abruptly after the onset of darkness. As I say, Ronnie never seemed particularly religious, but the dark shadows converging on our little camp seemed first to touch and then ignite a deep devotion in him. He casually mentioned to no one in particular that he had grown quite fond of attending church, and only wished services were held more often, maybe three or four times a week. I myself had always been religious, and now became fervently so, but I thought it might be well to mention aloud that I only passed through the ladies' underwear section in the Sears & Roebuck catalogue on my way to the sporting goods, just in case there might be some misunderstanding about impure thoughts and all that.

"Me too," said Ronnie. "Man, I flip right through the ladies' underwear section fast as I can."

It's quite possible that if we had remained in our little camp much longer, both Ronnie and I might easily have qualified for sainthood by no later than midnight. I could tell, however, that the darkness had started to stretch Ronnie's faith pretty thin. He was winding up his internal spring and settling his feet into the starting blocks. Then, without so much as a good-bye, he released the spring and shot himself toward home, leaving our blankets snapping up in the air like window shades.

Never had I seen such a disgusting display of sheer cowardice in one of my friends. Well, that was just something Ronnie would have to live with for the next forty years. Now, of course, there was no point in my remaining in camp alone, and so I reluctantly got up and calmly headed off toward home, my steady, woodsmanlike pace interrupted only by an occasional ricochet off the odd tree.

As I came in for a landing at home base, I miscalculated my elevation, overshot the back porch—and collided head-on with a large, humpbacked figure rounding the corner of the house. The creature made a hideous sound and leaped in the air, even as it flailed madly at me with both arms.

"Git back! Git back!" it cried hoarsely. "Wha . . . ? Is thet you, Patrick? Gol-dang, you skeered the livin' daylights outta me! What you doin' out this time of night?"

I was still inhaling, not a good idea when in that close a proximity to none other than—Rancid Crabtree!

"Rancid! For gosh sakes, what are you doing here?"

"Not a dang thang! Ah was jist passin' through," he said hoarsely. He reached down and picked up the gunnysack he'd been carrying over his shoulder.

"Oh, it's you, isn't it?"

"Ah look like somebody else to you?"

"I mean, you're the one who's been leaving the venison on our back porch, aren't you?"

"So what if Ah is?"

"Well, it's fine. It's great. I guess you shoot a deer every so often and then share it with us. That's nice."

"Ah don't shoot no deer. Thet'd be poachin'. What kind of no-good, miserable skonk you thank Ah am?"

"But the meat . . ."

"Oh, thet. Ah jist picks thet up along the highway, any poor critter what's too slow or too stupid to git out of the way of a car."

"You mean it's . . . it's *roadkill?*"

"Shore. But it be all good meat. Ah don't take nothin' thet's too ripe or all squished up."

"Dogs? Cats? Porcupines?"

"Whatever. Sometimes even a deer. Ah ain't heard no complaints about it. Now, you keep your yap shut about seein' me tonight. This is a secret jist 'tween you and me, hear?"

"Sure."

"Good. Now, here's your 'venison,' " he said hoarsely. "Put it over thar on the porch. And you dang well better act surprised when your ma finds it."

"Okay. By the way, how come your voice is so hoarse, Rancid?"

"'Cause you made me swaller maw chaw of tobacky, thet's why!"

The very next evening Mom burst out of the kitchen with a big platter of pancakes and another of steak.

"Oh boy, venison again!" cried Troll.

"Yes, indeed," Mom said. "Our secret benefactor struck again last night. Here, Patrick, take some venison and pass it to your sister."

"No thanks," I said, passing the platter on. "By golly, if I don't have the strangest hankering for leftover 'roast beef' tonight. Sounds really good to me for some reason."

It wasn't that I didn't think Rancid's, uh, 'venison' might not be good. I just wanted to wait awhile and see if Ronnie's dog, Sparky, turned up okay.

The Fly Rod

You see this fine old split-bamboo fly rod? Pretty nice, huh? I got it from Henry P. Grogan. Henry P. was the proprietor of Grogan's War Surplus back when I was a kid growing up in the little town of Blight, Idaho. Gosh, even now I can see Grogan's in all its splendor and glory, just as if it were yesterday instead of half a century ago. The storefront itself was elegantly decorated with ammo boxes, jerry cans, camouflage netting, a limp yellow life raft, and various other residue of recent history. It was nice.

On the lot next to the store, Grogan had carefully arranged the rusting wreckage of a dozen or so military vehicles in such a way as to conceal what had once been an unsightly patch of wildflowers. Most interesting of the vehicles was a Sherman tank. My friend Crazy Eddie Muldoon and I would have loved to get our hands on that tank, but Grogan refused to let us have it. He said it would be irresponsible of him to let two ten-year-old boys drive off though town in a Sherman tank, unless, of course, they somehow happened to come up with the cash to buy it. Grogan had a strict rule about selling dangerous war surplus to kids. You had to be a certain height—tall enough to reach up and put the cash on the counter—before he'd let you leave with the goods.

I was Grogan's best customer—he always said so, anyway—and over the years he and I worked out this special arrangement. He for his part would try to sell me every rotten, rusty, worthless piece of junk he had in the store. I would buy it. We both thought the arrangement quite equitable, he possibly somewhat more than I. Long before I reached my teens, my bedroom began to look like a miniature version of Grogan's War Surplus. Except for my mother's objections, I probably could have invaded a small country all by myself.

One day I was poking around Grogan's with the vague intention of buying another Eisenhower jacket, the military garment most favored by General Eisenhower during the war. So many boys at school wore them, recess looked like a convention of miniature Eisenhowers. While I was sorting through a pile of jackets in search of one that approached my size, Grogan yelled at me.

"Gol-dang it, Patrick, don't be scattering them jackets all over the floor! I try to keep this place neat. Now pick 'em up and throw 'em back up on the heap like you found them."

I glanced over at Grogan to determine his degree of irritation. Sometimes he got so upset he'd toss me out of the store, unless I was quick enough to wave cash at him. The sight of cash always seemed to have a calming effect on Grogan. On this occasion, however, he seemed well short of the boiling point. His beady eyes were blinking normally and hadn't disappeared into hard little slits in his grizzled face. Also, he was still puffing on his stub of cigar, a good indicator of his mood. While I was doing these calculations on his temper, I suddenly noticed something for the first time. On the wall behind the counter was an old but beautiful split-bamboo fly rod.

"Wow!" I exclaimed. "How much you want for that fly rod, Mr. Grogan?"

He turned and looked at the rod. "Ain't for sale."

"But you always say everything you got is for sale, including your wife, children, and pets."

"Well, I made a mistake. The rod ain't for sale. My policy still holds for the wife and children, though. Right now I'll let my son Junior go at half price. And I'll even throw in the pets to boot."

"Nope. What I want is that rod."

"You can't have it. But how about a nice flamethrower? Every fourth-grader needs a flamethrower. Great for starting campfires. Don't have to bother with kindlin' or nothin'. Drop a few chunks of wood on the ground, and, whoosh, you gotcherself one heck of a campfire."

The years passed. I grew up and went off to college. Whenever I was in town, though, I'd stop by Grogan's for a little shopping and to hone my bartering skills on its owner. No longer a kid wet behind the ears, I was now more than a match for Henry P. He and I would have a good laugh over all the useless junk he had foisted off on me over the years. Then he would try to sell me some rusty old war relic he had reserved just for me, but I would only chuckle, shake my head, and start to walk away. Then I'd stop. "Oh," I'd say. "I'd still buy that fly rod, though."

"Ain't for sale," he'd growl. "Junior, however . . ."

And that's how it went. Eventually, almost without

knowing it, I acquired a job, wife, kids, house, mortgage, "the full catastrophe," as Zorba the Greek used to say. Grogan in the meantime prospered. The old frame building of Grogan's War Surplus was replaced with a concrete-block edifice topped by a huge neon sign proclaiming the establishment as GROGAN'S EMPORIUM. Clerks now roamed the well-lit aisles, and clothing was arranged neatly in racks instead of in heaps on the floor, and there was not so much as a helmet liner or bayonet in sight. Personally, I found the new Grogan's—"The finest retail store in all of Blight!"—to be boring and even kind of sad. All the old character of the original Grogan's had vanished, as had Grogan himself. He now whiled away the later years of his life on golf courses and cruise ships and in fancy restaurants and resorts. As I say, it was sad.

On the rare occasions that I ran into Grogan on the street, his face would instantly light up and he would try to sell me something. "Have I ever got a bargain for you, Patrick! Look at this watch. Cost me a thousand dollars in Hong Kong. Fifty bucks and it's yours."

"It doesn't run."

"Probably just needs batteries."

"I don't think so. But I'll tell you what, Henry P. If you still have that fly rod, I'll buy it off you for fifty bucks."

"Fifty bucks! Ha! Nope. Ain't for sale."

It gradually became clear to me that one of Grogan's final goals in life was to sell me one last piece of worthless junk, just for old times' sake and the arrangement we had struck between us so many years ago. Then he'd die happy. For that very reason, I was determined not to be outfoxed ever again by the old fox. Let him die sad like everybody else, I thought cruelly.

One day my wife, Bun, and I were preparing to move to a new house. While we were cleaning out the basement,

Bun came across a pile of boxes in one corner. She opened one and drew back in amazement. "Good heavens, what is this junk?"

"Oh that," I said. "It's just a bunch of old war surplus stuff I bought as a kid. Don't know why I held on to it all these years."

She opened one of the larger cartons. Her face screwed up in disgust. "If you wanted to keep it, you should have stored it better. It's all rotten and rusty."

"Actually, it was that way when I bought it. We'll just toss it all out."

"The flamethrower, too?"

"Naw, not the flamethrower. I heard once it's good for starting campfires."

I hadn't even thought of Grogan in a long while, but suddenly I was flooded with fond memories of the old curmudgeon and decided to give him a call sometime. But before I could do so, he called me.

"Patrick, my old adversary! It's so good to hear your voice!" He sounded strange.

"How you doing, Henry P.?"

"Not so good. My string is just about run out. I'm in this dratted hospital, and I thought maybe you'd stop by for a visit. If you hurry, I'll try to hold on till you get here."

I was shocked. Somehow, I'd always thought of Grogan as living forever. I rushed over to the hospital.

Grogan appeared to be asleep in his bed. I hoped he was *asleep*. I gently shook his shoulder. Much to my relief, he opened his eyes.

"Patrick!" he croaked weakly. "You made it in time. I'm still here!"

"Henry P., I'm so sorry to see you like this."

"Never mind," he whispered. "We all got to go sometime. I just wish it was you and not me. Ha! Anyway, I got this for you." He groped over the side of the bed and hauled up—the fly rod!

"Here," he said. "I want you to have it."

Instantly overcome with emotion, I managed to choke out my thanks.

"You don't have to thank me," he said, wearily closing his eyes. "I know it's something you always wanted."

"But it's such a wonderful gift!"

Grogan's beady little eyes popped open. "Gift? What you mean, *gift?* That'll be two hundred dollars!"

"Two hundred dollars!" I gasped. "This rod is practically worn out!"

"Take it or leave it," he croaked.

"All I've got on me is a hundred and fifty and some change. Uh, how about a check?"

"You've sharpened up real good, kid, trying to pull that old check ploy on a dying man." He sank weakly back into his pillow. "I'll take the hundred and fifty. And the change."

I gave him the money.

"Just like old times, ain't it?" he said, managing a faint cackle.

My face twitched. "Yeah, it sure feels like it."

With a satisfied sigh, Henry P. Grogan closed his eyes and drifted off, a smile on his face.

On my way out of the hospital, I met his doctor and asked how much longer Henry P. had.

"A couple hours at most," the doc said.

"What was it?" I asked.

"The liver."

"Bad liver, huh?"

"Yes. Or it might have been the onions. If the old fox had enough sense not to eat liver and onions at Gert's Gas 'N' Grub, he wouldn't have to come in here and get his stomach pumped. Anyway, he'll be released in a couple of hours and—hey, steady there, man! Are you all right?"

"What? Oh, sorry. Yes, I'm fine."

"Well, I see Grogan sold you a split-bamboo fly rod. Too bad. He sold me one just like it. I think he has them made and aged by the gross in Hong Kong. Take my word for it, they're a worthless piece of junk. Wonder what sucker gave him the idea for this scam."

"It's hard to say," I said. "Very hard."

The Stupidity Alarm

(Whoa! Is that me beeping again?)

I don't know about you, but my world seems filled with alarms—alarms to warn me of smoke, fire, carbon monoxide, burglars, computer malfunction, car lights left on, keys left in the ignition, seat belts unfastened, doors not closed, and on and on. Unfortunately, I still lack one of the most important alarms of all—the Stupidity Alarm.

I hear a rumor that our technogeniuses finally got around to inventing one. It's about time. Just think of all the problems we'll avoid when we have an alarm to warn us every time we start to do something stupid.

The way it works, the Stupidity Alarm is implanted in an otherwise useless part of your body (I now have several available), and it has a series of warning signals calibrated to the degree of stupidity about to be engaged in. For modest stupidity, the alarm will go *beep-beep-beep;* for medium stupidity, *boop-boop-boop;* and for major stupidity, *WHOOOOP-WHOOOOP-WHOOOOP!*

Example of modest stupidity:

"By golly, I think I will have a third serving of that delicious chili."

Alarm: *Beep! Beep! Beep!*

Example of medium stupidity:

"Gee, Mr. Salesman, from what you say I probably should take the extended warranty on this toaster, which you're pretty sure will explode ten minutes after the regular warranty runs out."

Alarm: *Boop! Boop! Boop! Boop!*

Example of major stupidity:

"I guess I can read the fine print later. Where do I sign?"

Alarm: *WHOOOOP! WHOOOOP! WHOOOOP!*

When I think of all the times a Stupidity Alarm could have saved me from committing a stupidity, it makes me sick. Life would have been so much simpler. Here's one instance that comes to mind.

My children: "Daddy, please buy us a horse! Please, please, please, please!"

Me: "Well, kids, I guess a horse wouldn't be all that much trouble."

Stupidity Alarm: *WHOOOOP! WHOOOOP! WHOOOOP!*

The cowboy who sold me the horse said it loved children. That was true. But as I belatedly discovered, it hated adults. As we dickered over the price of the nag, I happened to notice that the cowboy had a bad limp.

"War injury," he explained.

One of his ears looked as if a bite had been taken out of it.

"Birth defect," he explained.

A plaster cast enveloped one of his arms.

"Car wreck," he explained. "Now, as I was saying, this here horse is real fine with children. That's why, out of the goodness of my heart, I'm letting you have him so cheap. I think every kid should have a horse. We got a deal?"

"You bet!"

WHOOOOP! WHOOOOP! WHOOOOP!

The kids named the horse Huck. After we'd had the horse for a while and I had observed how gentle it was with children, I saw no reason I couldn't use good ole Huck for pack trips into the mountain.

WHOOOOP! WHOOOOP! WHOOOOP!

I will omit the story of that pack trip, because it contains extreme violence, offensive language, and even some partial nudity, if having one's clothes ripped off on brush, trees, and rocks fits the nudity category.

Of course, not all the stupid acts I've committed have been major. Most are minor. I should mention here that my wife, Bun, didn't care too much for my idea of buying myself a Stupidity Alarm.

"I couldn't stand you *beep*ing and *boop*ing about the house all day," she said.

Well there you go. It was stupid of me even to tell her about the alarm, particularly when I know she just can't resist an opening for a bit of sarcasm. See, if I'd already had a Stupidity Alarm, it would have *beep*ed as soon as I thought about telling her my idea.

The Stupidity Alarm should be particularly handy for outdoorsmen—no offense.

"Hey, Pat, this road really looks terrible. Let's turn back."

"You kidding me or what, Joe? Ha! We haven't even kicked into four-wheel drive yet!"

Boop! Boop! Boop! Boop!

"Whoa! That road looks a lot worse than I first thought, Joe!"

The Stupidity Alarm could even save me from serious injury.

"Don't worry about that Vicious Dog sign, Ed. Farmers put those up just to scare off guys too timid to walk up and knock on the door and ask permission to hunt. Means the hunting is practically untouched. Watch me. I'll show you how it's done."

WHOOOOP! WHOOOOP! WHOOOOP!

"Uh-oh, my leg cramp's back. Guess you'll have to go ask the farmer's permission, Ed."

Or the Stupidity Alarm could save taking out a second mortgage on the house.

"I've been thinking about a nice inexpensive form of relaxation. Guess I'll take up bass fishing. Buy myself a rod, a couple of lures, that should about do it."

Beep! Beep! Beep!

Or it could save me from ridiculous sales pitches.

"Gee, Mr. Salesman, from what you tell me, I probably should buy the extended warranty on this thirty-thousand-dollar bass boat, which you expect to explode ten minutes after the regular warranty runs out."

Beep! Beep! Beep!

Or save me from serious gastric disorder.

Designated Camp Cook (guy who drew the short straw): "Either you guys agree to wash the dishes, chop all the firewood, clean my rifle, grease my boots, knock the snow off the tent, take baths in the creek, and let me deal the cards tonight, or I'm serving the hash again."

"But the hash has turned green and is starting to pulsate!"

"That's right."

"Tastes good, though. We'll have the hash."

WHOOOOP! WHOOOOP! WHOOOOP!

Actually, I suppose I don't have too much need for the Stupidity Alarm these days, but many decades ago it would have come in handy.

Here are a few instances.

Age eight and not likely to make it to nine—Crazy Eddie Muldoon has designed and built a deep-sea-diving outfit. The description of the outfit is too technical for the layman to understand, but I will mention that the helmet consisted of a milk bucket.

Eddie: "And guess what, Pat. You get to do the test dive! Don't that sound like fun?"

Me: "Gee, thanks, Eddie!"

Age nine—Eddie and I have built an airplane at the peak of a steep barn roof. It's a glider, actually, because we can't figure out how to get the motor out of his mom's gas-powered washing machine. The glider will zoom down the barn roof until it has picked up enough speed to loft it up into the air. Neato!

Eddie: "Guess what, Pat. You get to be the test pilot. Don't that sound like fun?"

Me: "No way, Eddie! It's too dangerous. You must think I'm stupid. But I'll ride along as copilot."

Age sixteen—my friend Retch Sweeney and I have hiked far back into a trackless wilderness. It's difficult to imagine two more astute woodsmen.

Retch: "I'm starving. We probably shouldn't have eaten all our food the first two days."

Me: "Now we think of that! Well, maybe we can live off the land."

Retch: "We could if we knew how to eat moss. Hey, look at those storm clouds boiling up over those mountains. Maybe we better not camp on this ridge."

Me: "What are the chances that of all the places lightning can strike, that it would hit right in our camp? Ha! This ridge is as safe as anywhere."

As a point of interest, when lightning strikes right in the middle of your camp, it's very much like being inside an exploding bomb, with fire going every which way and you going every which way, and the bolts are trying to hit you and turn you into a Crispy Critter, but the bolts fail to lead you enough because you are moving so fast.

Age twenty-five—Retch Sweeney and I are already experienced white-water rafters.

Retch: "It's a good thing we ran into that kindly old rancher who knows all about the river. Otherwise we'd keep worrying about how bad everybody says The Narrows are."

Me: "Yeah, it was nice of the kindly old rancher to tell us that the danger of shooting The Narrows is greatly exaggerated. You can always trust kindly old ranchers to give you the straight dope."

As another point of interest, I should mention that some kindly old ranchers can turn out to be homicidal maniacs in disguise.

Looking back over more decades than I care to mention, I guess I'm actually pretty happy Stupidity Alarms hadn't been invented when I was younger. If they had been, I probably would have spent my life doing only wise things, and we all know how boring that can be. Anyway, it's too late for me to change now, even after I get my Stupidity Alarm. As a matter of fact, I'm even thinking about buying another horse, so I can use it to pack into high mountain lakes and things. I just hope I can find one that likes adults and isn't spooked by a whole lot of *beep*ing, *boop*ing, and *WHOOOOP*ing.

Work
and Other Horrors

Of all the adults I knew, the two I most wanted to be like when I grew up were my Uncle Flynn and Rancid Crabtree.

Rancid lived in a little shack back in the mountains behind our farm and never did a lick of work. That seemed to me like a sensible way to live, the kind of career I hoped to find for myself.

I had noticed early in life that most of the adults I knew loved work, because that was about all they ever did. Work. Work. Work. If they lost one job, they rushed frantically about in search of another and wouldn't be satisfied until they found one. They weren't choosy about what the job was, either. If it consisted of carrying logs on their shoulders from the bottom of a mountain to the top twelve hours a day, seven days a week, why, they would be delighted with it, for no other reason than it was a job. They obviously loved work in all its forms, and no matter how hard and dirty and mean a new job might be, they spoke highly and even glowingly of it, as if they'd found some grand prize.

Every so often I'd get carried away by their enthusiasm and try a little work myself, as an experiment, to see if I could detect the pleasure in it. But I never found any. As far as I could tell, Rancid had been right all along. Work merely used up the time one might otherwise spend fishing and hunting—or resting up for fishing and hunting. I was never sure which Rancid enjoyed more, the hunting and fishing or the resting up for. He was an expert at both.

My Uncle Flynn didn't work either, but he was much different from Rancid. He was tall and slim and handsome and always wore nice clothes: shiny shoes and nifty suits, white shirts and little bow ties. He smelled nice, too, whereas Rancid, on his best days, simply smelled. Uncle Flynn spent his time playing poker, smoking cigars, and chatting with his pals down at Pig Weed's Saloon, and he always seemed to have lots of beautiful girlfriends. He usually had lots of money, too. There seemed to be some connection between lots of money and lots of beautiful girlfriends, but I couldn't figure out what it was. I thought no work and lots of money was a lifestyle that probably suited me best, and I wanted to study Uncle Flynn more to see how he managed to come up with that particular combination.

My mother often predicted that Uncle Flynn would come to a bad end, but as far as I could tell he was having a pretty darn good middle. Even though he didn't work, Uncle Flynn from time to time went off on long vacations. One time while he was on an extended vacation, some of his friends came around looking for him. I was only about eight at the time, and I don't know why they thought I could keep track of my uncle.

Crazy Eddie Muldoon and I had been out picking up

empty beer bottles and cigarette butts along the highway. We sold the empties at Pig's saloon and saved up the butts until we had enough to smoke, not realizing back then that cigarettes could be bad for our health. A big black sedan passed us, squealed to a stop, and backed up. The car had four men in it. Eddie and I dropped our bottles and cigarette butts and ran down into the ditch. A man in a suit got out of the backseat, leaving the door open, as if he might have to make a fast getaway. Eddie picked up a good throwing rock, just in case. The man stuck his hands up and smiled at Eddie. Then he looked down at our sack of empties and the little pile of cigarette butts.

"I see you boys are out collecting empties and cigarette butts," he said. "Very industrious."

"Yeah," I said. "We just collect the cigarette butts, we don't smoke them. It's a hobby."

"And a very good hobby, too," the man said. "Might be worth a lot of money someday. Speaking of money, I was wondering, Pat, if you'd seen your Uncle Flynn around. He skipped out—uh—kind of disappeared for a while, and we were just wondering if you might have seen him lately."

I looked at the other man sitting in the backseat. "What do you want him for, to play baseball?"

"Baseball?" the man said. He glanced over his shoulder at the car's backseat, where his friend was holding a base-ball bat on his lap. "Exactly right! We were getting a little game together this afternoon and needed Flynn to pitch, ain't that right, Charlie?"

"That's right," Charlie said. "To pitch."

"Can't somebody else pitch?" I said.

"No," the man said. "Flynn's got the ball. We need to get the ball back."

"Well, I haven't seen him in a couple of weeks. He said

he was going on a long vacation. But if I do see him, I'll be glad to mention you're looking for him."

"Don't bother. I expect he knows."

After the men had roared off in their black sedan, Eddie and I wandered over to Rancid Crabtree's shack to see if we could talk the old woodsman into giving us a ride down to Pig's saloon so we could sell our empties. Usually, Eddie and I just walked into his shack without knocking, because there was no danger of ever catching Rancid indisposed, like in the bathtub, for example, or changing his clothes. He had this theory that soap and water would eat holes in your protective crust and let the germs get in. In regard to clothes, he thought taking them off when he went to bed was a waste of time, because he'd just have to put them back on again in the morning. It made sense. But today the door was locked. Eddie pounded on it. That was when we heard the burglar alarm go off—namely, the sound of a shell being jacked into a 12-gauge pump shotgun. We looked at each other. What was going on? Rancid never locked his door, never had reason to alarm burglars.

"Who's thar?" the old woodman shouted.

"It's just me and Eddie," I shouted back.

Rancid opened the door a crack, stuck his head out, and looked around. "So what you two want?"

"We want you to drive us to Pig's so we can sell our empties."

"Cain't."

"Well, at least let us come in and rest."

"Cain't."

"How come?"

"'Cause I got a visitor, thet's how come. Now beat it, the two of you."

"Oh," I said to Eddie. "He's got Ginger Ann in there, I bet."

Ginger Ann was Rancid's lady friend, at least when she

wasn't fighting with him. She owned the Tin Horn Ranch and ran it all by herself. The Tin Horn looked a lot like Rancid's place, except on a larger scale. I was glad that Rancid and Ginger Ann had made up. Their latest fight had been going on for most of a year.

Then we heard a man's voice. "Oh what the heck, Rance, let 'em come in. Maybe they have some news from the outside world."

I recognized the voice right off. It was Uncle Flynn's! He was sitting at the table, his hands wrapped around Rancid's spare coffee mug. His shirt was dirty, his hair uncombed, and he had started growing a beard. He looked terrible.

"What are you doing here, Uncle Flynn?" I gasped.

"Yeah," Crazy Eddie said. "You look terrible."

"Thanks, Eddie," Uncle Flynn said. "Actually, I'm just taking a little vacation."

"At Rancid's shack?"

"Yep. Oh, I did think about Mexico and even South America, but then I said to myself, 'By golly, I'll just go stay with Rancid for a spell.' I wanted a place with some atmosphere, and as you can tell, this little cabin has a *whole lot* of atmosphere."

"Thanks, Flynn," Rancid said. "Ah'm glad you like it."

"You're welcome, Rance. In fact, I don't think I'd be up to even a bit more atmosphere. So what brings my favorite nephew and his sidekick out here?"

"Nothing much. But guess what, Uncle Flynn, some men in a big black sedan are looking for you. They stopped and talked to us up on the highway. They had a baseball bat with them but said you had the ball. They said they need you to pitch."

"Don't worry, Flynn, they ain't gonna find you here," Rancid said.

"How come you don't want them to find you?" Eddie asked. "It sounds like fun."

"Not as much as you might think, Eddie," Uncle Flynn said. "You see, I lost the ball. It was their ball. They would be very upset."

"You didn't tell me about the ball," Rancid said. "I thought it was jist thar money you lost?"

"That, too."

"Oh," I said.

"You mean you lost their money?" Eddie said. "How did you do that?"

"A slight miscalculation. But no problem, Eddie, I can get the money back. All I need is a small stake and a patsy."

Eddie and I both knew what a small steak was, but we'd never heard of a patsy, unless maybe it was a girl. Rancid apparently was familiar with both. "By dang," he said, pounding the table. "Why didn't Ah thank of this before? Ginger Ann's got a ton of money and ain't adverse to an occasional wager. She an ornery old cuss, but she'd jump at the chance to do a little gamblin'."

"Poker?"

"Naw, we need to come up with a contest of some kind thet she thinks she can win. You let her win a few rounds until she gets overconfident. Then you bet all the rest of your money and take her to the cleaners. It'd sarve her right, her thankin' she's so durn smart and all. Take her down a notch or two."

"One problem, Rance," Uncle Flynn said. "I'm flat broke."

"I hear they're hiring down at the mines right now," Crazy Eddie said.

Both Uncle Flynn and Rancid shuddered. "You watch your mouth, Eddie!" Rancid growled. "Ah don't like to hear talk like thet!"

"Me either," Uncle Flynn said. "You must have picked up that trashy language from Pat's mother. Sounds about like her."

"Ah'll tell you what, Flynn," Rancid said. "Ah got maw life's savin's buried out in the yard in a quart jar. Ah'll loan it to you, and you can pay me back and a bit more from the winnin's."

"I appreciate the offer, Rance, but I couldn't possibly risk your life's savings."

"Ha! Thar ain't no risk. You see, Ginger Ann thanks she can outshoot me, but she cain't. You jist asked the boys hyar if Ah ain't the best dang shot in the valley."

"That's right," I said. "They don't even allow Rancid in the turkey shoots anymore. He shows up, they give him a turkey and he goes home."

"Nobody can touch Rancid when it comes to shooting," Crazy Eddie said.

"Gosh, I don't know," Uncle Flynn said. "How much do you have in your life's savings, Rance?"

"Eighteen dollars."

Uncle Flynn looked thoughtful. "And you say she has plenty of money, this Ginger Ann? I wouldn't want to cause her any hardship."

"Don't you worry about thet. If she put all her money in the bank, her mattress would be flatter'n a pancake."

"Hmmmm. Well, if we handle this just right, Rance, I might be able to pick up the cash I need. But I'm not going to take advantage of the poor woman. Anything I win I'm going to consider a loan and pay it back to her. How are we going to work this, anyway?"

"Wahl, like this. You bet her a dollar a shot and Ah'll let her win the first three or four rounds. Then you bet our whole wad. And Ah'll beat her. But she'll jist thank thet was a lucky shot. Then Ah'll let her win a few more and—"

"I know the drill," Uncle Flynn said. "Let's do it!"

"Hot dang!"

Uncle Flynn combed his hair, shaved, and put on a clean shirt. Rancid took his twenty-two out in the yard, stuck a wooden match in a log, stepped back about fifty feet, and shot the match in two.

"Shucks," he said. "Missed."

"What do you mean, 'missed'?" Crazy Eddie shouted. "That's the greatest shot I've ever seen!"

"Thanks. But you see, Eddie, I was aimin' to light the match."

"Holy smokes!"

"Rance is just joshin' you, Eddie," I said.

"Mebby, mebby not. Anyways, you two younguns stay here at the shack and don't you breathe a word to nobody that Flynn is bunkin' hyar. You could git hart real bad."

"Gee, you think those men would hurt us, Rance?"

"Ah don't reckon they's thet mean. But Ah am!"

After Rancid and Uncle Flynn headed up the trail toward the Tin Horn Ranch, Eddie and I went in the shack and dug out Rancid's checkerboard and started playing checkers.

"I feel kind of sorry for Ginger Ann," Eddie said.

"I don't," I said. "Didn't you hear Uncle Flynn say he would pay her back all the money he won?"

"Sure."

"Well, Uncle Flynn is a man of his word, Eddie, and pretty darn often, too."

A couple hours later, we heard Rancid and Uncle Flynn laughing as they came back down the trail. We ran out into the yard. Uncle Flynn had a wad of cash in his hand.

"I got to hand it to you, Rance, you're one of the best shots I've ever seen."

"Ah reckon thet's true."

"Yep, no doubt about it. And Ginger Ann's the other best shot I've ever seen."

"She's a good cook, too. You hear her invite me up for supper tomorrow night. I guess thet means we're made up. Hot dang!"

"Sounds like it to me."

"And you was afraid we might lose maw life's savin's, Flynn. Ha!"

"Well, we certainly could have, Rance. But when I saw Ginger Ann light that match with her first shot, I knew it was time to fold 'em."

"Ah probably could have taken her in the long haul, but it would've been too close fer comfort. You shore seventeen dollars will do you, Flynn?"

"This will do me fine, Rance. I'll pay you back first chance I get."

Eddie and I could scarcely believe what we were hearing. Ginger Ann had actually outshot Rancid and won a dollar off Uncle Flynn.

"Wahl, Ah got to go down to the crick and git cl-cl-cleaned up for supper with Ginger Ann," Rancid said. "Thet woman is so dang picky!"

"I thought supper wasn't until tomorrow night, Rance," Uncle Flynn said.

"It ain't. But it usually takes me two days to git cl-cl-cleaned up. It's a hideous chore, but Ah's got to do it."

Uncle Flynn sat down on Rancid's chopping block, dug out a cigar stub he'd wrapped up in a piece of paper, and, emitting a long sigh, lit it. Eddie and I walked over to him.

"Gosh, what are you going to do now, Uncle Flynn?" I asked.

"You know how your mom always said I'd come to a bad end, Patrick. Well, I guess this is it."

"No!" I shouted. "Not that! Those men won't ever find you, Uncle Flynn!"

"That's not the bad end. Tonight I'm driving down to the mines and going to w-w-work."

"No!" I shouted. "Not that!"

The Dangers of Light Tackle

Many years ago, I gave a speech, "Whither the Moose," at an Oregon seaside resort. As the audience hung on my every word, a chap in the first row suddenly lost his grip and fell into a deep slumber, dragging most of the row after him. Even though I was only two hours into my speech, I decided to relinquish the microphone to the next speaker, who had been trying to wrest it from me for some moments anyway. One of the secrets of successful public speaking is to recognize the subtle signs of ebbing attentiveness in the audience, and then to wrap up the talk as quickly as possible, which I did forthwith and to resounding applause, if I may be so immodest as to mention that. Making my way toward the nearest exit, I noticed a couple of friends of mine, Flick and Benny, standing by the door. Flick beckoned me over.

"Pat, guess what!" he said. "We managed to charter a little salmon fishing boat for this afternoon and wondered if you wanted to go along."

"Naw," I said. "I have no interest in catching little salmon."

"You don't understand. The boat's little, the salmon are big!"

"In that case, I'd go, but I don't have any tackle with me."

"The tackle is all taken care of. Good sturdy salmon rigs."

An hour later we met at the boat, which wasn't as small as I'd been led to believe. Four people could fish out of it comfortably without fear of tangling lines, except when a fish was hooked, of course, and then all other lines would have to be reeled in—no big problem, or so it seemed at the moment. Ned, the burly, bearded boat captain, was setting out the salmon rigs, big sturdy rods, massive reels, line strong enough to land Brahman bulls. My heart leaped up. Clearly, Ned was a captain accustomed to bringing in big fish.

"You fellows about ready?" Ned called out.

"Got one more guy coming," Flick replied. "He'll be here any minute."

"I thought it was just the three of us," I said.

"Nope," Flick said. "Figured it would be better if we split the cost of the charter four ways instead of three. Besides, Wiggens is a nice guy. Met him last night during the cocktail hour. Oh, there he is now, I bet."

A classy red sports car sped into the marina and slid to a stop, its motor rumbling expensively. A thirty-something fellow got out, slender, handsome, thick wavy blond hair, top-of-the-line fishing togs, clearly the kind of successful and confident individual who inspires instant hatred.

"Wow, would you look at that car!" Benny said. "What a lucky guy. Car, looks, clothes, money. Cripes, why can't I be like him!"

"'Cause you're short, fat, bald, and poor," Flick said. "Otherwise, no reason."

"Some people have it all," I said. "Their worst day is probably one of the best for most of us."

"No kidding," Flick said. "Some guys are just naturally lucky, no doubt about it. He'll probably haul in some monstrous salmon, and the rest of us won't get so much as a nibble."

Flick introduced us and we shook hands all around.

"Just call me Wiggy," Wiggens said. "Or Wig for short."

Clearly, it was not enough that Wig was one of the luckiest people on earth; he also had to be a regular guy. One of the things I've noticed about rich people, most of them tend to be nice. It's very irritating. You would think that out of common decency they would at least allow us the satisfaction of not liking them. But no, they have to be nice.

The time would soon come, however, when Flick, Benny, and I would regard Wig with undiluted hate.

"What you got in the fine leather cases there, Wig?" Benny asked.

"Oh, just my rod and reel and some tackle," Wig said. "I like to use my own stuff." He opened one of the fine leather cases and began setting up his rod.

"Hey, that's real nice," Flick said, frowning. "But don't you think it's kind of light for salmon?"

"I like to use light tackle," Wig said. "It seems more sporting. No offense to you guys."

"Yeah, sporting," Benny said. "I like sporting."

Half an hour later we were a couple of miles offshore, the sea like undulating blue silk flecked with diamonds—

ugly, but fishermen can't always expect nice dull gray choppy water.

"Let's give her a try," Ned said. "Picked up a couple of real nice chinook right along through here yesterday."

Wig had his line out before Flick, Benny, and I had even started to bait up. Flick stepped over and nudged me. "You see that weird fly Wig tied on? Man, I was going to say something to him, but I thought he might get embarrassed. When he don't catch anything in an hour or so, I think maybe I'll just suggest that he—"

"Fish on!" Ned shouted. "Wig's got a good un. Look at that baby take out line. Wheweeeee! Lucky thing you other fellers hadn't put in yet. We'd had us a fine tangle of line with this light tackle Wig's usin'."

It took a good half hour for Wig to work the salmon up close to the boat, but it was exciting to watch. We all cheered him on.

"Way to go, Wig!"

"All right, man!"

"Nice job! You almost got him now, Wig!"

Ned got the net and stood poised to scoop up the fish. "Oh, nice! This baby will go over twenty-five pounds or I miss my guess . . . !"

Bzzzzzzzzzzzzzzzzzzz . . . !

The salmon took out a mile and a half of line.

Flick, Benny, and I walked to the far side of the boat's tiny cabin and sat down on the deck. Flick bit off a chaw of tobacco and Benny lit up his pipe. I thought about delivering them a lecture on the threats to their health of these nasty habits but, glancing at their faces, decided that the lecture might be an even greater threat to my health. We sat in sullen silence for another forty-five minutes or so. Then we heard Ned say, "Easy! Easy, Wig! Don't horse it. Easy. Just a bit more and I can get the net under . . . !"

We leaped to our feet, ready to cheer.

Bzzzzzzzzzzzzzzzzzzzzzzzzzzzzz . . . !

We sank back down on the deck. A chill wind was coming out of the north, and a nice chop had built up on the gray water.

"Either of you guys bring an extra jacket?" Benny asked, hugging himself.

"Didn't even bring one," Flick said.

"Me neither," I said. "Thought it was going to be warm."

"Never even notice the cold when I'm catchin' fish," Flick said. "I could be coated with ice and never even notice it, when I'm catchin' fish."

"Fishin's funny that way," Benny said. "I got this bad back, pains me something awful, but if I'm catchin' fish, it don't bother me no more than a mosquito bite. It's killin' me now, though."

"How about giving me a few puffs on your pipe there, Benny?" I said.

"Can't. Way things are goin' I might not have enough tobacco to last out till Wig gets his dang fish in the boat."

"Let's at least go sit in the cabin," I said.

"Can't," Flick said. "Ned's got it crammed with stuff."

Then we heard Ned again. "C'mon, don't pamper that fish! Horse him in here, dang it! Just thumb that spool and give a big jerk! I'm freezing to death . . . !"

We started to get up.

Bzzzzzzzzzzzzzz . . . !

We sank back down.

Flick fired a round of tobacco juice over the side of the boat. "You know what I think? I think we oughta rush over there and cut Wig's line, that's what I think."

Benny groaned and rubbed his back. "Too late for that. We've gone past the point of just cutting his line. I think we should break that flimsy little rod of his and throw it overboard!"

"Yeah, that's a good idea," Flick said. "And then we could throw Wig in after it!"

"That would be murder," I said.

"So?" Flick said. "What's your point?"

"We might get caught," I said. "A coast guard boat is pulling up astern."

A voice boomed out from a speaker on the coast guard boat. "Are you fellows in trouble?"

"No!" Ned yelled back.

"Then what are you doing out in the dark in this storm?"

"Trying to bring in a fish on light tackle!" Ned screamed back.

"Oh," the voice boomed. "Well, we better stand by until you get the fish in, because the waves are starting to build up."

The waves were coming at us from the side and the boat was rising and dropping and dropping, and rising . . .

"Wig's light tackle is threatenin' our lives," Flick said, as a wave hit the side of the boat and sent icy spray over us. "I say we rush him right now and cut his line."

Then we heard Ned yell. "Got it netted! Fish on board!"

We struggled to our feet. "Boy, am I going to give Wig a piece of my mind about his light tackle," Flick growled.

"Me too," Benny snarled. "When I get done chewing on him he ain't ever gonna want to fish again!"

"Got a few unkind words for him myself," I said, as we groped our way around the cabin. "I can't believe he actually brought that fish in on light tackle. The kind of *luck* some guys have!"

Ned had a light shining on the fish, a big silvery chinook. Wig stood there staring solemnly down at his salmon. His face was pale from exhaustion, his eyes almost teary as he looked up at us.

"I got something to say to you, Wig!" Flick said. "And that is, by—"

But Wig didn't seem to be listening.

"Finally!" he blurted out, interrupting Flick in mid-oath. *"Finally something worked out right for me this year! Finally!"*

Flick, Benny, and I stared silently at Wig, then at the fish, then at one another, then at Ned. Ned stared back at us. He gave a small shake of his head. Maybe Wig wasn't such a lucky guy after all, if catching a fish was the first thing to work out right for him that year. And it was already September!

After a few seconds, Wig said, "I'm sorry, I interrupted you, Flick. What were you about to say?"

"Me? Oh, I was just gonna say, 'By gosh, that's a mighty fine fish, Wig.'"

"Yeah, it's a beaut," Benny put in. "Hard to imagine you could catch a big fish like that on such l-l-l-light tackle."

"Best salmon I've seen all year," I said. "Congratulations, Wig!"

"Thanks, guys," Wig said. Then he went back to looking solemnly at his salmon.

The coast guard boat followed us in, our boat bucking and crashing over the waves and throwing us about.

"You know somethin' strange?" Flick said, smiling. "I don't feel cold at all anymore."

"Me neither," I said.

"My back still hurts like crazy," Benny said.

"You wimp!" Flick said. "We was tryin' to have a poignant moment here!"

Faint Heart

Third grade, Delmore Blight Grade School. Once again our teacher, Miss Deets, had come up with one of her horrible ideas, this one undoubtedly intended to embarrass me as much as possible. Miss Deets was rich. I couldn't ever remember her wearing the same dress two days in a row. Why, I figured she must have as many as four or five nice dresses, maybe even more, and she owned at least two pairs of high-heeled shoes, one black and the other white. She wore jewelry, too, lots of it, and she had these little holes punched right through her ears, which she covered up with earrings. Personally, I thought the holes in her ears were rather gruesome, but I never mentioned it to her, because I thought they might be some kind of birth defect. I certainly wouldn't want to call attention to a person's birth defect.

Not only was Miss Deets rich, she was beautiful as well. And she always smelled really nice, not all that common among folks in our part of the country. So her smell was something that distinguished her all by itself. I probably could have loved Miss Deets, and even did for a while. But then she started coming up with all these ideas designed to embarrass me. And this latest one, why, it was one of the worst yet.

"Class, I have just had the most wonderful idea," Miss Deets announced. "I want each of you to bring in your father and have him tell all about the kind of work he does. I'm sure your fathers' employers will give them a few hours off from work to participate in this project. It will be exceedingly educational for all of you and give you some excellent insights into all the exciting and productive careers available to you."

A murmur ran through the class, casting some doubt on the excellence of this idea. I didn't join in the murmur. I was frantic. I didn't know what I could do. Finally, I raised my hand.

"Yes, Patrick?"

"I'm sorry, Miss Deets, but I can't bring my dad in."

"Well, you haven't even tried yet, have you? I'm sure that whatever your father is doing he can get a little time off to visit the class."

"He can't."

"And just why are you so sure about that, Patrick?"

"He's dead. Died two and a half years ago."

"Oh, I see. I'm sorry to hear that."

I thought I was off the hook, and Dad, too. I figured he'd rather be dead than have to come in and talk to Miss Deets's third-grade class.

"But I have a contingency for those of you whose fathers are, uh, unavailable," Miss Deets went on. For a moment, my spirits leaped up, until I discovered that a contingency wasn't a gift of some kind. "No, those of you whose fathers are unavailable must bring in another adult, an uncle, perhaps, or a close friend of the family, to tell about whatever it is they do for a living. And I will accept no excuses!"

Well, I was in it now. I had only two choices. There was my Uncle Flynn, of course, who could come in and tell about his gambling, and that would have been very interesting to the class as a possible career choice, but recently Uncle Flynn had had to leave town abruptly, so abruptly he hadn't even stopped to pack. That left only the old woodsman Rancid Crabtree, my mentor in all things related to the outdoors and life in general.

Right after school that day I raced over to Rancid's shack. Mostly what Rancid did was hunt and fish, but he also trapped on occasion, and I thought he could tell my fellow third-graders about trapping. Rancid was out sitting on his chopping block, apparently thinking about splitting some wood. He never did any kind of work without thinking about it long and hard first, just in case it turned out to be a foolish notion. He seemed glad to see me.

"Patrick, good to see you, boy." He shot a spurt of tobacco juice at a scruffy chicken wandering past, missed, then wiped his mouth on his sleeve. "What brings you up this way?"

"I got a terrible favor to ask, Rance."

"Ah hope it don't involve money."

"Nope. It's really awful."

"Wahl, spit it out."

"Our teacher, Miss Deets, well, she says we have to bring in our dad or another man to tell what he does for a living. And I picked you!"

"Nope, cain't do it. Ah'm tied up thet day."

"I haven't told you the day yet!"

"Don't matter. Ah'm tied up thet day. Otherwise, Ah'd do it jist fer you. By the way, this teacher, this Miss Deets, what's she look like?"

"Oh, she's beautiful, Rance. And rich, too."

"Rich, too. Sounds an awful lot like maw kinda woman."

"And she smells good!"

"Smells good! This is gettin' better 'n' better. Wahl, gosh-dang, mebby Ah can shuffle maw schedule around on thet day. Ah thank Ah jist had a cancellation. Yes sirree, Ah reckon Ah'll be able to oblige you after all, Patrick."

"Thanks, Rance. But I haven't told you the terrible part of the favor yet."

"Tell me the tarrible part."

"You'll have to take a bath!"

"A bath! Ah'll be gol-dang if thar ain't always a catch! Ah 'spect you wants me to shave, too, an' mebby even comb maw har!"

Over the next few weeks, the fathers came in one by one to tell what they did for a living. I have to admit, they were all pretty interesting.

Mr. Skaggs: "I work in the woods. Run a chain saw and fall trees. I suppose some of you kids is wondering why I only have three fingers on my left hand. Well, you ain't never seen so much blood. Just barely missed gettin' gutted by that saw. Way it happened . . ."

Mr. Carson: "I work in the woods. Run a skidder. Now, I suppose you kids are wondering what happened to my face. Well, one day . . ."

Mr. Haverstead: "I farm. Go to work at four in the morning and quit about ten at night, but it ain't always that easy. During calving time, I put in pretty long days."

Mr. Kojak: "I work in the mines. Maybe some of you kids are thinking about working in the mines. In that case, you better study real hard and get good grades and go off to college. *Because you'd be dang fools to work in the mines!*"

And so on. Miss Deets didn't seem too happy with the reports from the fathers, but we kids found them very educational. Those lectures probably raised our grade average by several hundred percent.

Finally, the day arrived for Rancid to come in and give his report on what he did for a living. I have to admit I was more than a little nervous. I hoped he'd remembered about the bath. Then, right at the appointed time, the door to Delmore Blight third grade was flung open and in strode Rancid Crabtree. If anyone had had a feather handy, they could have knocked me flat on the floor with it.

Rancid had not only taken a bath—his face still appeared a bit raw from the scrubbing—but he had shaved and combed his hair, slicked it back with some bear grease, I imagine, and his sweeping mustache had not only been tamed but trained, and swept out expansively on both sides of his face. He wore a suit, a bit threadbare at the elbows, but clean and pressed. He was lean and tan and stood well over six feet tall in his gleaming cowboy boots. Far and away, Rancid was the most impressive and most handsome of the speakers so far. I couldn't have been more proud of him. And then he delivered his lecture.

"Yawl wants to know what Ah does fer work? Wahl, Ah'll tell you. Ah don't do none! Not a gol-dang bit! Ah fishes and Ah hunts whenever I wants to, goes to bed when Ah wants to, and gits up when Ah wants to. Ah even takes baths when Ah wants to, and Ah 'most never wants to. Ah ain't got nothin' agin honest work, nor dishonest work neither. It's work in general Ah'm agin. Fer as Ah can see, work jist uses up a man's life, when he could jist as well be out huntin' and fishin' and enjoyin' hissef. And Ah'll tell you this . . ."

Rancid's lecture set the class grade average back where it had been before. Probably lower. I doubt there was a boy in the class who wasn't considering Rancid's lifestyle as a serious career option. I know I was.

Riding home with Rancid after school, I raised a few of my concerns about his lecture.

"I don't think not doing any work at all was what Miss Deets expected you to tell the third grade," I said. "She looked pretty shocked."

"Thet's okay. The brats seem to enjoy it. Clapped and cheered fer me afterwards, didn't they? Mebby Ah helped shape some of their miserable little lives. Thet's what teachin's fer, ain't it?"

"Yeah, I guess so, Rance. You certainly shaped my life. You did really well, no matter what Miss Deets might think. But then you did that awful thing right in front of the whole class!"

"Ah did? Must've jist slipped out without me noticin'. Gol-dang, Ah gots to be more mindful of thet than Ah'm out in public."

"Oh no, you know what you did! You asked Miss Deets would she go to the Saturday dance with you! I was horrified! She was too!"

"Ha! Kinder give her a shock, all right. Put a little color in her cheeks, too. But like Ah keeps tellin' you, boy, faint heart never won fair maiden. It don't hurt to try. All can happin is, you git turned down."

"Yeah, I suppose you're right. But that isn't what horrified me."

"It ain't?"

"No! What horrified me is, she *accepted!*"

Mrs. Peabody II

Retch Sweeney and I were grounded during our freshman year in high school, not by parental decree but because our mountain car, Mrs. Peabody, had perished. We had named the car after our favorite high school teacher, an honor we were sure she cherished, although obviously not enough to show her appreciation in the form of higher grades. We weren't surprised by her failure to reciprocate, but it had been worth a shot.

Mrs. Peabody, the car, could not have been more lovely—something, by the way, that also could be said for the teacher after whom we'd named the vehicle. We had practically stolen the car from Budge Honeycut, owner of a local wrecking yard. Budge said so himself, wetting his thumb and counting out the wad of forty $1 bills we'd handed over. He even went so far as to say that he'd never run into two sharpies as shrewd as Retch and I. "Shucks," he said, "if every client was like you fellas, I'd likely go broke in no time at all."

Three months after the purchase, Mrs. Peabody blew up, not something you'd expect from a $40 car. Budge Honey-cut admitted as much. He said we must have forgotten to put oil in it. That wasn't true. When we mentioned to someone that we got twenty miles to the gallon, we were talking about oil, not gas. Retch suggested to Budge that he might want to give us a refund on the car, but that was a danger-ous thing to suggest. When you make a man Budge's age laugh that hard, he could easily have a heart attack. But I've written about the Peabody tragedy in *Never Sniff a Gift Fish*, and it would make me too sad to dwell further on it here.

Six months later, we had scraped together another $40. A neighbor had an old junker out in his back lot, and he said he reckoned he might be able to let it go for $100. We told him we had only $40 and change. "How much change?" he asked. "Sold!"

For $40, of course, we didn't expect any of the usual automotive accessories, such as doors, fenders, headlights, taillights, a complete floor, or a backseat. But the car had all the essentials, like a motor and wheels and, uh, well, a motor and wheels. It did have brakes, too, which quite of-ten actually worked. We always drove the car flat out, or about fifteen miles an hour. That may not seem like much in this speed-crazed age, but it was a lot better than pedal-ing a bike up into the mountains with all your camping gear tied on behind.

As soon as we'd made the purchase, we rushed into Mrs. Peabody's classroom and told her we were naming our new car after her, too. She said, "Be still, my heart." So we knew she was pleased, although probably not enough to affect our grades.

As with our first car, naming the vehicle after our English teacher apparently resulted in a certain amount of confusion in our small town of Blight. The possibility of such confusion never occurred to Retch or me, of course. Otherwise, we'd probably have named the car something else.

A mechanic by the name of Heck Ramsey owned a little gas station and garage outside of town, and occasionally we'd wheedle him into diagnosing some malfunction of our car and, with a bit of luck on our part, fixing it. We stopped by Heck's garage one day for just such a purpose. He came out of the shop wiping his hands on an oily rag, taking care to conceal his joy over another visit from us.

"What you two want now?" he growled. "Don't you see I'm busy?"

"We don't want to bother you, Heck," Retch said. "Just stopped by for a cold pop and to chew the rag a bit. Oh, by the way, here's something that will interest you. Mrs. Peabody's got a bad exhaust problem."

"I got one myself," Heck said, "but I can live with it. I expect she can, too."

"Yeah," I said, "but it's us we're worried about. We're afraid the fumes will kill us. Our eyes start to burn and get all watery, and we can hardly breathe."

"Sounds like a real bad case all right, about the worst I ever heard of. Mrs. Peabody, you say?"

"Yep, Mrs. Peabody. Say, Heck," I wheedled, "you don't happen to have an old tailpipe around that you could install on our car, do you?"

"What's wrong with the tailpipe you got?"

"Probably nothing. Except it's up on the Pack River road someplace."

"I'd be glad to solve that little problem for you."

"You would? That's great!"

"Yup. What I advise is, you drive with your heads out

the winders, 'cause I shore ain't installing a tailpipe on it."

"She don't have windows," Retch pointed out. "Doors neither. But the exhaust comes right up through the floor."

"Oh, well, I suppose I could put on an old tailpipe. But I ain't doin' the job for free. How much money you got?"

"A dollar and fifteen cents."

"Just enough. Drive her up on the rack."

Retch and I hung around the garage picking up a few new swearwords while the greedy mechanic installed the tailpipe.

"You'd think he could've left us with at least enough change for a couple bottles of pop," Retch muttered.

"You know mechanics," I said. "Take every last dime you have."

Mechanics weren't the only persons to give us problems over Mrs. Peabody II. Sheriff O'Reilly was always after us, too. We were tooling up the highway one day at fifteen miles an hour, minding our own business, when once again we noticed a red light blinking faintly through the cloud of black exhaust smoke boiling out of our new tailpipe. While we were discussing the possible source of the light, the faint sound of a siren rose above the roar and the periodic explosions emanating from Mrs. Peabody's engine.

We pulled over and drifted to a stop, not wanting to use up what was left of the brakes unnecessarily. Because I was the passenger, it was my job to stick my feet down through a hole in the floor and skid them along the ground to help with the braking. Retch had constructed an anchor we could drop through the hole, in case of an emergency, but we hadn't yet had an emergency.

Presently, the sheriff stuck his head through the window, or what would have been a window if Mrs. Peabody had possessed any. We tried to interest him in casual conversation, but he didn't appear in the mood, or so we judged from his shouting into Retch's ear, which he had grasped between two fingers and pulled up close to his lips.

"I thought I was done with you two idiots after your last hazardous heap blew up," he bellowed. "Listen to me, Retch Sweeney! If I catch you and Pat out on the highway one more time with this death trap of a monstrosity, I'm going to run both of you in! I'm going to lock you up in a cell and feed you nothing but bread and water for a year! You hear me?"

We laughed. Sheriff O'Reilly was such a kidder.

The sheriff gave Retch's ear a fierce little tug. "One more thing! You got to get a license for this pile of junk!"

Retch and I were deeply offended. It was one thing to hear Mrs. Peabody called a "death trap," but "pile of junk" was downright insulting, particularly when you consider that I have purified the sheriff's vocabulary somewhat.

"What for we need a license?" Retch said.

"So the vehicle can be identified, that's what for!"

"You didn't have no trouble identifying it, did you, Sheriff?" Retch said.

It's always a bad idea to jest with a law officer when he has hold of your ear. Retch was still yelping as I tried to placate the sheriff with some good news about our car.

"Guess what, Sheriff?" I said. "Mrs. Peabody got her exhaust problem cured."

"*Exhaust* problem? Oh yeah, Heck Ramsey mentioned it to me. Said it was the worst case he'd ever heard of. And by golly, if *Heck* says so, I got to believe it was downright terrible. Thank goodness she's cured. A thing like that can knock the devil out of your social life."

"Yeah," I said. I didn't mention that Retch and I had very little social life anyway.

"Well, you boys get this heap off the highway and don't let me catch you out here again."

"Uh, one more thing, Sheriff," Retch said, trying to work his ear back into its original shape. "How about giving us a boost to get started? That way we won't have to get out and crank her."

One of the things I hated worst about the sheriff was that long, cold, silent stare. It could lift the hairs on the back of your neck.

We managed to avoid the sheriff most of the time. Fortunately, we had to drive only about three miles down the highway to get to a road that took us up into the mountains. No one ever bothered us or Mrs. Peabody when we were up in the mountains. That's one of the things I've always loved about the mountains. Oh, occasionally, when we had Mrs. Peabody parked alongside the road, a logging truck would stop and the driver would yell out the window, "You boys dang lucky you didn't get kilt. That's the worst accident I ever seen."

Loggers have a cruel sense of humor.

During the six months or so we had her, Mrs. Peabody II served us faithfully, hauling us hither and yon on fishing and camping trips and just wandering about on the mountain roads. But then one day, tragically, she conked out.

We were up near the end of the Pack River road and practically flying down a steep hill. I was skidding my feet as much as I could stand, and Retch was yelling, "Throw out the anchor! Throw out the anchor!" But then, suddenly, all the working innards of Mrs. Peabody seized up and the car came to a grinding, shuddering halt. As if that weren't bad enough, a fire broke out in the engine compartment. We doused the flames with sand, but it was too late to save her. She was done for. Retch theorized that she had blown a gasket, although neither of us was quite sure what a gasket was or if Mrs. Peabody possessed one. It sounded good, though. Sadly, we started the long walk home.

Presently, a logging truck came by and picked us up. We rode along in silence.

"You boys look a bit down in the mouth," the logger said. "Can't be all that bad. What's the problem?"

"We just lost Mrs. Peabody," Retch said. "She's dead as a doornail."

"Mrs. Peabody! Good heavens! I didn't even know she was sick. Must have happened just like that."

"Yeah," I said. "It was pretty sudden. Something went haywire with her innards."

"Oh, that is just so terrible," the logger said. "She was such a beauty, too."

"We thought so," Retch said.

"I doubt she was a day over thirty," the logger said, shaking his head.

I was surprised the logger would think our car so old, but I didn't see any point in correcting him.

The logger shook his head sadly. "Come to think of it, I did hear from the sheriff she had some serious kind of, uh, gastric problem. Probably had something to do with it."

"I reckon so," Retch said. "She blew a gasket."

"Good grief!"

The very next week Retch and I stayed after class to break the bad news to Mrs. Peabody about the demise of her namesake. I thought she took it rather well, judging from the way she leaped into the air and clicked her high heels together.

Cereal Crime

Of all the crime fighters in our county, none was more dedicated than Crazy Eddie Muldoon. Everyone said so. His reputation was based on the fact that Eddie had single-handedly eaten about five thousand boxes of Yum-Yum cereal in order to qualify for The Famous Detective Crime-Solving Kit. Other kids, myself included, had tried for the crime-solving kit, too, but not one of us made it through a single box of Yum-Yums. They were bad. I guess the cereal company's idea was, if you could eat that much Yum-Yums, you had proved you were tough enough to be a crime solver.

Six weeks had passed since Eddie had mailed the cereal company his five thousand box tops, along with a quarter for postage and handling, and we were beginning to suspect the Yum-Yum people of a crime of their own, stealing

Eddie's quarter. Then one day Eddie came running into my yard.

"It finally came!" he yelled. "Now I can start solving crimes!

"Wow!" I cried, glancing about. "Where is it"

"I got it right here in my pocket."

"In your pocket?" I had expected the crime-solving kit to be at least larger than a deck of cards. The illustration on the Yum-Yum box had implied the kit might be some-what larger, possibly of a magnitude requiring delivery by a freight truck.

"Yeah," Eddie said. "Look at this!" He pulled a flat black box from the bib pocket of his overalls and from it extracted a gleaming badge with the words "Junior Detective" clearly discernible, if you held it up close to your eyes and tilted it so the light hit it just right. I could feel an envy shade of green creeping over me.

"And this here is my detective identification card," Eddie said, holding up a piece of paper quite a bit larger than a postage stamp. His name was printed on the card. I recognized his printing, with "Eddie Mul" neatly penciled across the top of the card and "doon" running down the right edge. Clearly, the ID cards were intended for detectives with short names. Eddie reached into the box again.

"Tah-tahhh!" He held up a gleaming pair of handcuffs. "Aren't they great!"

They *were* great! Real handcuffs! They looked as though they might work, too, if you apprehended fairly small suspects. But that was no problem. There were lots of small suspects around in serious need of apprehension.

"But here's the best part of all," cried Eddie. "Tah-*tahhh!*" He held up a magnifying glass, its lens easily the size of a dime.

By now I was little more than a green quivering mass of

envy and shame. Why hadn't I had the ambition and forti-
tude to eat five thousand boxes of Yum-Yums so that I, too,
could have acquired a Famous Detective Crime-Solving Kit!

Crazy Eddie instantly sensed my disappointment and,
taking only a few moments to savor it, said, "Don't feel
bad, Pat. You can be my assistant crime solver."

"Really, Eddie? You really mean it?"

"Sure."

"And I get to use your handcuffs and magnifying
glass?"

"No."

Eddie said I could watch him solve crimes, though, and
that was certainly better than nothing. Not much better
than nothing, but, as Eddie astutely pointed out, beggars
can't be choosers.

Eddie and I immediately went out looking for crimes to
solve. He said the first thing we had to do was round up
some suspects.

"Don't we have to find a crime first?" I asked.

"It works either way," Eddie explained. "First you find
the suspect and then you figure out what he did."

"How do you know he did anything?"

"Well, he wouldn't be a suspect then, would he?"

"I guess not," I admitted. Eddie clearly was already a
master of deduction. "What do we do with the suspects
after we've rounded them up?" I asked.

"Oh, we get them all together in a big room, and then
I go around and irrigate them one by one."

"You irrigate them? How do you irrigate them?"

"Don't you ever listen to Sid Sleuth on the radio? He's
always irrigating suspects. It's easy. You just ask them a
bunch of questions. Pretty soon one of them slips up. He
says something like, 'I didn't shoot the victim.' And then
Sid Sleuth says, 'Ha! How did you know the victim was

shot? I never mentioned that he was shot. You're going to get the chair.' "

"What chair?"

"It doesn't matter what chair, dummy. There's always a chair of some kind around. By the way, it might be a good idea for you to call me Sid Sleuth."

"I'm not going to call you Sid Sleuth, Eddie."

"I'll let you use my magnifying glass."

"So, Sid Sleuth, do you have any suspects in mind?"

"Just one. Rancid Crabtree."

"Rancid? How come Rancid is a suspect?"

"Mostly because he's handy," Eddie said. "Let's go over to his shack and I'll irrigate him."

Rancid was sitting on his chopping block smoking his old corncob pipe as we approached.

"I see he smokes a corncob pipe," Eddie whispered. "Very interesting. Jot that down."

"I don't have anything to jot it down with."

"Remember it, then."

"Okay." It would be pretty easy to remember, because Rancid always smoked a corncob pipe.

Rancid studied us with a good deal more suspicion than we did him. "So, what in tarnation brings you two over hyar? Ah 'spect it's got somethin' to do with ruinin' maw day."

"I'm investigating crimes, Mr. Crabtree, and I have a few questions to ask you," Eddie said. "Here's my Famous Detective Identification Card."

Rancid squinted at the card. " 'Eddie Mul,' " he read aloud and then tilted his head sideways, " 'doon.' Ah guess thet's you all right, Eddie. So what questions you want to ask me?"

"First, where were you on the night of the crime?"

"What crime is thet, Eddie? Am Ah a suspect?"

"Yes."

"Oh. Wahl, let's see, exactly what night was the crime committed?"

Eddie looked at me. "What night was the crime, Pat?"

"I can't remember, Sid Sleuth. Last week sometime."

"Wahl, you're barkin' up the wrong tree, Eddie," said the old woodsman, "'cause Ah was home here in maw shack ever night last week."

"Any witnesses?"

"Jist one."

"Who was that?"

"Me. All Ah had to do was look down, and thar Ah was, right whar Ah was supposed to be, ever night."

"I guess that clears you, then, Mr. Crabtree. Thanks for your time."

"Don't mention it, Eddie. Ah shore hopes you find the person who committed the crime."

"Aha!" cried Eddie. "So, you know a crime was committed! What was it?"

"Thet's what Ah'm tryin' to find out!"

"Hmmm," Eddie said. "Just as I suspected. Well, goodbye, Mr. Crabtree. I have more detective work to do. And remember not to commit any crimes. Otherwise you might get the chair."

"Ah could use a chair. All Ah got to sit on now is a couple blocks of firewood. What kind of chair is it?"

Eddie thought for a moment. "Just a chair."

Over the next few days Eddie irrigated every suspect within three miles of his house but was unable to turn up a single crime. All the neighbors knew what Eddie had suffered through to collect his five thousand Yum-Yum box tops, and they told him they were real sorry they hadn't committed any crimes for him to solve, or even had crimes committed against them. His failure to turn up a single crime was beginning to tell on Eddie. He'd become cross and jumpy, and excitement no longer sparkled in his eyes. For the first time since I'd known him, he seemed drained of enthusiasm. Here he had downed enough Yum-Yums to fill a silo, and for what? His crime-solving kit had proved totally worthless without any crimes to solve. Now he just moped about his house and was no fun at all. Even his mother said she was worried about him. As for myself, I was about ready to start looking for a new best friend.

"Something's wrong with Eddie," I told Rancid Crabtree one day. "He hasn't been able to find any crimes to solve, and now he won't come out to play or anything. He just mopes about."

"Ah'm sorry to hear thet. It be jist a dang shame we don't have more crime in these parts. Now let me thank on this a bit. Mebby Ah did hyar of a crime? By gosh, Ah did! You know thet daft old Mrs. Swisher lives up the road, nutty as a fruitcake, and always callin' the sheriff on me 'cause she thanks Ah'm in cahoots with Satin and the like? Shoot, if Ah was making deals with the devil, Ah'd at least have a chair to sit on. Anyways, Swisher, she's got a rusty old milk bucket on her front porch thet she filled up with dirt and planted to flowers, thet's jist how crazy she is. Can you imagine such a thang? Ha! What Ah heard happened was, somebody snuck up in the middle of the night and stole thet bucket of flowers, though why somebody would want it beats the heck outta me. Mebby Eddie could try to solve thet crime."

"Rancid, that's it! We've finally got a real crime!"

"Yep. It shore does look like it."

I rushed over to Eddie's house. He was out in his backyard and looked about as miserable as I'd ever seen him.

"Eddie! Eddie! A crime has been committed!"

He leaped to his feet, instantly transformed. "Where?"

"Old Mrs. Swisher's. Somebody stole that bucket of flowers off her porch!"

"Great! This is really great, Pat! Wait till I tell Mom. Then I'll go solve the crime!"

We rushed into the house and told Mrs. Muldoon that Eddie had a crime to solve.

"Oh, I'm so glad!" she said, throwing her arms up in the air. "What is it?"

"Somebody stole that bucket of flowers off Mrs. Swisher's porch."

Mrs. Muldoon's smile faded. "Eddie, I hate to tell you this, but I stopped by Mrs. Swisher's not more than an hour ago, and that bucket of flowers was right there on her porch. I even commented on how pretty it was. There must be some mistake."

Eddie's whole body sagged.

"Gee, I'm sorry, Eddie," I said. "I was sure a crime had been committed."

"It's okay," he said sadly. "I guess I ate all those Y-Y-Yum-Yums for nothing. We ain't never going to have a crime for me to solve."

But Eddie was wrong, because the weirdest thing happened. The very next morning daft old Mrs. Swisher drove into the Muldoon yard. She was furious. Somebody had sneaked into her yard the night before and stolen her bucket of flowers right off her porch! She was on her way into town to report the theft to the sheriff, but, she said, she doubted it would do much good, because the sheriff hardly even bothered to investigate her complaints about Rancid Crabtree being in cahoots with the devil.

"Oh, that is so wonder—I mean, *awful!*" Mrs. Muldoon blurted out. "Eddie! Eddie! Come quick! A crime has been committed!"

Eddie grabbed his crime-solving kit and we ran all the way over to Mrs. Swisher's place to investigate.

"The first thing we got to do is look for clues," Eddie explained. He got out his magnifying glass, lay down on his belly, and very carefully examined the spot where the bucket of flowers had been. "I don't see any fingerprints," he said. "This could be a tougher case than I thought. There don't seem to be any clues around."

"How about that corncob pipe?" I asked.

"Yeah," Eddie said. "How about that? I didn't even know Mrs. Swisher smoked, let alone a corncob . . . Wait just a darn minute!"

Half an hour later, we walked up to Rancid's cabin. There on his front porch was the bucket of flowers, just as Eddie had deduced. The old woodsman stood over it, sprinkling it with water.

"I caught you, Mr. Crabtree," Eddie announced. "You stole that flower bucket from Mrs. Swisher."

"Danged if you didn't catch me, Eddie. How'd you ever solve the case?"

"You made one fatal error, Mr. Crabtree. You left your pipe at the scene of the crime!"

"Drat! Ah was wonderin' what happened to thet pipe!"

An hour later, Eddie and I were lugging the flower bucket through Mrs. Swisher's gate.

"I just wished we could have handcuffed the criminal," Eddie said.

"Yeah," I said. "Too bad the cuffs would only fit around his thumbs."

The sheriff was leaning against a post on Mrs. Swisher's front porch, while she pointed with great agitation at the spot where the flower bucket had been. The sheriff was just stifling a yawn as we walked up.

"Good heavens!" Mrs. Swisher yelped at us. "You found my flower bucket! That is so wonderful, boys!" While she went to get her purse to give us a reward, a whole nickel as it turned out, Eddie told the sheriff how he'd solved the case.

"Mighty good work, son," the sheriff said. "So your big clue was that corncob pipe. Very interesting. Maybe I should start eating those Yum-Yums myself. Now that crime is starting to pick up around here, I probably will. I'm mighty thankful for the help on this case, Eddie. I may have to call on you again."

Well, that compliment inflated Eddie's head so much I expected his feet to float right up off the floor. Eddie didn't even mention my help in solving the crime, but, after all, he had done the hard part—he had eaten the Yum-Yums.

"Do you think Mr. Crabtree will get the chair, Sheriff?" Eddie asked.

"The chair? Oh, yeah, no doubt about it."

Word spread like lightning among the neighbors about how Eddie Muldoon had solved his first case with his crime-solving kit, and everybody seemed pleased that Eddie hadn't eaten all those Yum-Yums for nothing.

A couple days later my mother drove me up to Rancid's shack. "I heard you were supposed to get the chair," she told him. "So I brought it up." She pulled the chair out of the trunk and handed it to the old woodsman.

"Why, thank you kindly, missus," he said. "Ah can use another chair, jist in case Ah ever gets company."

"Oh, I didn't know you had a chair already."

"Yup. Mrs. Muldoon brought me one. Thet makes three Ah got now."

"Three?"

"Yes, ma'am, it was the durndest thang—pardon maw

language—but the very day Eddie solved my crime, the sheriff pulls in the yard and gives me one of the chairs from the jail. Said he'd heard from Eddie Ah was supposed to get the chair, and he just wanted to make sure Ah did."

Pickers

This is the time when I most enjoy huckleberry picking—three feet of snow outside and the wind howling out of the north. It is much more enjoyable to sit by a warm fire and think about picking huckleberries than actually to pick huckleberries. August is the usual time for huckleberry picking, except then there is the real possibility that you might actually have to go out and pick huckleberries.

There's much talk around here about picking huckleberries. A reporter stopped by Gert's Gas 'N' Grub a while back and tried to interview some of the men sitting around over lunch about a recent shooting. But, as the reporter said in her story, all the men wanted to talk about was picking huckleberries. Talking about picking huckleberries is a local art form, at least among the male population. It's a test of a man's woodsmanship to find huckleberries even in a bad year for huckleberries. That is why there is almost never a good year for huckleberries, because then even city folk could find them.

"Bad year for huckleberries," Ben says.

"Not if you know where to find them," Joe says. "Got three gallon last Sunday."

"Got four gallon myself," Ben says. "All of 'em big as marbles."

"Mine was the size of grapes," Joe says. "Never seen such big huckleberries. The bushes was so loaded with berries they laid over on the ground."

Joe's statement is true. He really never has seen such big huckleberries, including those he just got. It is also important to note that both Ben and Joe say they "got" huckleberries. They are careful not to say that they *picked* the huckleberries. Their wives picked the huckleberries and that is how they *got* them. Ben and Joe spent their time scouting around over the mountain in search of the mythical patch with berries the size of grapes. That is how picking huckleberries is done and has been done for thousands of years. It's the natural order of things.

Over the years, my wife, Bun, and I have developed a system for picking huckleberries. I drive her up to a fairly decent patch in the mountains, and she sits right down and begins to pick, the berries playing a little tune as they *plink-plink-plunk* into the bottom of her bucket. It takes a great deal of patience and about three million huckleberries to fill a gallon bucket.

"These berries are great," Bun says. "Why don't you pick right here?"

"You think these berries are great?" I say. "There's got to be better berries than these around. I'll do a little scouting."

So I go off scouting. What I'm looking for is something on the order of a huckleberry patch I discovered when I was sixteen years old and camped out near the falls on

Pack River. The berries were as big as grapes, and so thick the bushes lay over on the ground. I picked my hat full in five minutes. Once you've known a patch like that, you can never settle for anything less. And that is why I scout while Bun picks. By the time I've covered a mountainside and returned, Bun has her bucket full.

"Find it?" Bun asks. She knows about the legendary patch, the unattainable patch.

"Nope," I say. Then we drive home. Bun's berries are enough for a pie and some huckleberry pancakes, maybe even some huckleberry muffins. I usually wish we had got more huckleberries, but that would have meant . . . I can't bring myself to say it.

That, at least, was our huckleberry picking for many years. Then Dave Russell showed me his huckleberry picker and allowed as how it enabled him to pick about eighteen gallons in an hour.

"Really?" I said.

"Well, a gallon anyway."

A gallon is a lot of huckleberries to pick in an hour. The best I'd done at that point was a gallon in ten years. But I'd done a lot of scouting, and that's not something to be scoffed at. If I could pick a gallon in an hour, well then, I might get serious about picking. I studied Dave's picker very carefully and then went home and built one of my own, pretty much along the same lines, although mine was a bit more cumbersome and somewhat less attractive. It consisted of a wooden box with nails studded straight out along the mouth of the thing—"The Thing," that's what Bun called it—but the idea was basically the same as Dave's. The principle of the picker was right, if not the details. The principle was that the nails would serve as little claws to rake the berries off the bush and into the box. It didn't work worth a darn.

Dave had got me interested in huckleberry pickers,

though, and a little while later I was poking around a local farm store and came across a commercial huckleberry picker. I took it home and showed it to Bun, who was much relieved she'd never have to be seen with "The Thing" anymore. We immediately rushed off to the mountains to pick huckleberries. The new picker was a marvel, and in scarcely more than four hours I'd picked a whole half gallon of huckleberries—and leaves and twigs and assorted insects. It made me proud.

A short while later we went huckleberry picking with my brother-in-law, Dolph, and his wife, Norma, Bun's sister. Dolph fancies himself a pretty fast picker (a city person for many years now, he's forgotten about scouting), but I beat him hands down with my little commercial picker.

"I don't think that picker's so hot," he said. "I can build a better picker than that."

"Can't," I said.

"Can," he said. "And I will. That thing of yours is just a tin can with wires on it."

Dolph happens to own a manufacturing company and has at his disposal huge metal chompers and benders and welders, and all kinds of computers to run the machines. So he put about a million dollars' worth of machinery to work creating his little huckleberry picker, probably the world's most expensive picker up to that time. He probably could have bought a Yugo for what that picker cost, but he was proud of it and couldn't wait to try it out. He was certain it would beat my picker. In the meantime I had bought a new picker, a fancier model, and this baby was fast! It left Dolph's picker in the dust.

"I'm not finished yet!" Dolph cried. He returned to his plant and set computers to humming and huge machines to slicing and welding and stamping, and out of this thundering and clanking roar popped another little huckleberry picker. This one was made out of some rare and expensive metal alloy, lithuanianium, I think, but I'm not sure. This baby was high tech. It looked as if it should be on the space shuttle, possibly to take over the controls in an emergency.

Sensing that Dolph's pickers were gaining on my pickers, I invested in several more commercial pickers.

Dolph's latest picker had me worried, but nevertheless I went off into the mountains with him, determined to push one of my new pickers to the utmost. I needn't have worried. His picker pulled ahead by a couple of gallons, but then it went crazy and began spitting berries over the top of his head. My picker soon closed the gap and then went on to win.

"Stop with all the huckleberries!" Bun shouted as I walked in the door. "We'll have to build on an addition just for huckleberries."

"There's more in the truck," I said.

I didn't hear from Dolph for several weeks, but I've known him for forty years and more, and I was certain he hadn't given up. And he hadn't.

The next time he showed up at my house, Dolph was pleased as punch. "Come out and look at my new picker," he said.

"Why didn't you bring it in?"

"Can't," he said. "The components are too big."

Components. This was serious. Huckleberry pickers aren't supposed to have components.

We went out and Dolph took the picker from the trunk of his car. This thing was weird. If I'd found it on the floor in my house, I'd have pushed it out the door with a stick. It looked like something you could be arrested for in some states.

"What is it?"

"It's the world's first electric huckleberry picker, that's what!"

"Electric? How are you going to power it up in the mountains?"

Dolph pointed to a portable generator in his trunk. It was surrounded by a huge coil of extension cord.

"The generator and extension cord are just for testing it out," he explained. "I still have to figure out a portable power source."

"I bet," I said. "Let's go down to Gert's Gas 'N' Grub and have a cup of coffee, and you can explain how it works."

We got a booth at Gert's and ordered coffee and donuts, donuts having a low potential for ptomaine poisoning. Dolph started explaining his latest invention.

"What I do is flip the *on* switch and these little steel fingers begin to vibrate, and they very gently vibrate the berries off the bush and into the container, without disturbing the leaves on the bush."

"Ha!" I said. "This is the most ridiculous thing I've ever heard! Vibrate the berries off the bush! You got to be kidding!"

"You're just jealous," Dolph said. "This baby is going to leave those little store-bought jobs of yours at the gate."

"Oh, yeah!" I said. "No way!"

Just then Gert walked over and served our coffee and donuts. "What are you boys gettin' so worked up about?"

"Oh, nothing," I said. "We were just comparing our pickers."

"I can't imagine that would be such a big deal," Gert said.

"Oh, it's just that we're having this little competition," I said, "to see which one is the fastest."

"Doesn't sound like something I'd want to risk money on," Gert said.

"Well, if you did," Dolph said, "you'd want to bet on mine. It's electric."

"An electric one," Gert said.

"Yeah, it's really pretty fantastic," Dolph said.

"I'll bet it is," Gert said.

"You want to see it?" Dolph said.

"Not really," Gert said.

"It vibrates," I said.

"I imagine so," Gert said. "Yours do anything special, Pat?"

"Naw," I said. "It's just a regular old-fashion one."

"Sometimes old-fashion is best," Gert said. "At least you don't have to worry about getting electrocuted."

About then Charlie Higgens walked in, and Gert called out to him. "Hey, Charlie, you ever hear of an electric huckleberry picker? This guy over here claims to have one."

For some reason I felt mildly disappointed, I suppose because Dolph's picker was getting all the attention.

Bun put her foot down and wouldn't allow me to pick any more huckleberries, so Dolph and Norma went without me. I didn't get to see the electric huckleberry picker field-tested, and I'm really sorry I didn't. According to Norma, who phoned later, the electric picker worked surprisingly well—for a while. But then the vibrations began to increase in intensity, going faster and faster, and the *off* switch failed to work, and the picker began to rattle and whine, and sparks were flying out of it, so Dolph couldn't put it down for fear of starting a forest fire, and then pieces of his picker began flying every which way, and finally—Norma was almost in tears at this point in her report—the picker disintegrated right in Dolph's hands, even as he was screaming at Norma, "P-p-p-p-p-pull th-th-th-th-th-the pl-pl-pl-pl-plug!"

The last I heard, Dolph was finally able to sleep nights without vibrating out of bed. Next summer, though, I know he will be back with an even more fantastic picker, maybe one equipped with its own atomic power plant. I doubt I'll go along to see that one tested either.

Well, lunch is ready and I'd better go eat. I hope we're not having huckleberries again.

My Fishing Trip
with Ernie

Many beginning anglers are unaware of the proper procedure for undertaking a fishing trip. As a service to them, I will now describe a recent fishing trip engaged in by my neighbor Ernie Beckman and me. Beginners will no doubt appreciate my effort to keep the technical detail to an absolute minimum, so as not to confuse them.

A few words about Ernie are appropriate. He's about seventy years old and amiably cantankerous, although not sufficiently so to be admitted to the Patrick McManus Curmudgeon Club, of which I am founder and president. But he is working on it. In fact, several times during our fishing trip he appeared to be reaching curmudgeon status. As far as I can determine, Ernie has spent most of his life having fun. He has been inducted into three different motorcycle-racing halls of fame. For thirty years or so he worked in television commercials, where most of his duties seemed to involve flying planes and cars, the cars at only a slightly lower altitude. So you would think Ernie's nerves would be immune to about any danger that might possibly occur. Had I thought differently, I certainly wouldn't have taken him along on a fishing trip with me.

Ernie and I have cabins on a river island upstream from a very big lake. Getting to the lake is no problem when the water is high. On this particular occasion, however, the water was low, very low, and in order to get to the lake it was necessary to follow the submerged and meandering channel out over the bar that has built up at the mouth of the river. This also is no problem, because I have memorized the half-mile-long meanderings of the channel.

"Remember," I told Ernie the night before the fishing trip, "we want to get started at five sharp in the morning."

"Okay," Ernie said. "I'll be ready."

What I forgot to tell Ernie is that experienced anglers like myself don't mean five sharp when they say "five sharp." They mean "somewhere around eight, or maybe ten." "Five sharp" is merely an expression used to impress inexperienced anglers or anyone who might be eavesdropping. It would sound terrible to say, "We'll head out somewhere around eight, or maybe ten." Your fishing license could be suspended for saying something like that.

Ernie, although an experienced fisherman, is unfamiliar with the high-tech fishing terminology of the McManus school of angling. He was up and ready to go at five sharp. While waiting for me to show up, he sat in his kitchen and drank a whole pot of coffee. Thus, his nerves were in terrible shape by the time I arrived, a condition I strive to arouse in all my fishing companions, because it produces the sharpness of reflexes for setting a hook at just the right instant. But little or no thanks do I get for that effort.

We piled into my boat and made ready to cast off. I

started the 90-horse motor before tilting it into the water. This raised Ernie several inches straight up off his seat, apparently giving him the impression the boat was about to explode, or had exploded. A whole pot of coffee will do that to you. But I could see his reflexes were sharp.

"Lower the motor!" he bellowed.

Well, of course I had planned on lowering the motor, because otherwise the prop would be out of the water and we wouldn't get anywhere.

"You got everything we need?" Ernie asked, rubbing circulation back into his ears.

Ernie apparently had heard from some of my other friends that I have a tendency to forget some little thing. I ran through my mental checklist. Coffee. Cookies. Potato chips. Orange slices. Peanuts. Tackle box. Sodas. Jacket. Caramel corn. Sunglasses. "Yes, I've got everything. You don't want to believe all the rumors you hear about me, Ernie."

"I should hope not," he said.

We headed down the river toward the mouth. As we approached the submerged gravel bar, Ernie went up to the bow so he could watch for snags.

"There's no need for that," I said, chuckling. "I know the mouth of this river like the back of my hand."

"Stop! Stop!" cried Ernie.

"What now?"

"Better check the back of your hand and find where the water's deeper than six inches!"

I greeted this report with very little enthusiasm, for it meant that we had strayed out of the channel, a result of Ernie's distracting me by waving his arms wildly and shouting incoherently. If Ernie and channels would just stay where they are supposed to be, one would avoid this problem. Now we would have to make our way through uncharted waters.

An hour later we had made it into the deep water of the lake. By then Ernie was hoarse from shouting, "Stop! Stop! Left! Left! Snag! Snag!" and so forth. This bit of excitement burned up most of his morning infusion of caffeine, and when he finally returned from the bow and slumped in his chair, he seemed all but mellow, the facial twitches gradually subsiding into epidermal calm.

After a bit, he said, "I'd better set up the downriggers. Where are the weights?"

"Didn't you put them in the boat?" I asked.

"Me!" he shouted. "Why should I put them in the boat? It's your boat! They're your downriggers!"

"Well, we'll just have to go get the weights," I said. "We can't fish today without downriggers."

An hour later we had traversed the bar twice more, but we now had the weights. Ernie's voice had eroded to a low croak from shouting about rocks and snags and generally making a nuisance of himself.

"Okay," he croaked. "I've got the downriggers hooked up. Hand me the rods."

"The rods?" I said. "Why, they're back by you."

"No, they're not!"

"They're not? Hey, Ernie, you're going to get a really big kick out of this. You know what?"

We made much better time crossing back and forth over the bar once again, and I felt I was starting to get the hang of navigating the mouth of the river at low water. I thought Ernie might even go so far as to compliment me on my nifty boat handling, but he merely slumped in his chair with a crazed look on his face. That's what happens when you drink too much coffee.

"Slow to trolling speed and I'll put out the lines," Ernie said after a bit.

"Put out the lines?" I said. "I'll tell you what, Ernie, I'm getting a little hungry. What say we run across the lake and have lunch at Dave's House of Fry? You know the place. It's got that sign that says, 'Fine Dining and Bait.' "

"I could use something to calm my nerves," Ernie said. "And I don't mean decaf. But we'd better not. Looks to me like there's a storm brewing off to the west, and we'd have an awful lot of open water to cross."

I couldn't help but laugh. "Ernie," I said, "you're talking to an old sea horse here. I can feel a storm in my bones, and I can tell you right now we have nothing to worry about."

"If you say so."

"I say so." We made the long run across the lake in record time, right up to the last two hundred yards to the dock in front of Dave's House of Fry.

"I always check the gas gauge on my boat before I head out onto the lake," Ernie said.

"Paddle a little faster," I said. "It will help you work up an appetite."

Dave's House of Fry was devoid of customers, except for Wolf Klaus, a huge logger we both knew. We chatted a bit with Wolf, who is a bit hard of hearing.

"How's Jake, Wolf?" I asked. Jake is his brother.

"The steak's fine," Wolf said. "Just a little on the tough side."

"Good to hear," I said.

"Why am I here? Oh, the boss made me take this first-aid course this morning. Missed out on a whole day of logging. Dang nuisance if you ask me, but it's company policy. Now I have to spent all afternoon in the second part of the course."

"Tell Ella I said 'Hi,'" I said. Ella's his wife.

"Ain't that the truth!"

Ernie and I took the next table over. "That Wolf can be a hard person to carry on a conversation with when he isn't wearing his hearing aid," I said.

"I know," Ernie said. "Wolf sure is big. Got arms on

him like telephone poles. I sure wouldn't want him to get mad at me."

We ordered the fried steak with fried potatoes, fried bread, and fried salad. "I haven't seen restaurant prices this cheap in years," I said. "I wonder how Dave makes any money."

"He makes it on the antacid tablets," Ernie said. "Probably charges five bucks apiece for them and they sell like hotcakes—fried hotcakes!"

I noticed that Ernie's voice was even more raspy now, apparently from his reaction to the boat running out of gas.

"Your voice is getting awfully croaky," I said.

"It's all your fault," Ernie croaked.

"Maybe the waitress can find something to soothe your throat," I said. "I'll ask her."

"Don't!" Ernie said. "Leave well enough—"

"It's the least I can do," I said, and then called out to the waitress. "Miss! Miss! My friend here is croaking! Could you—!"

"Choking!" shouted Wolf. "Good gosh a-mighty, Pat, he's probably got a chaw of meat stuck in his throat." He charged around the table and swept Ernie up in his arms, chair and all.

"Help!" croaked Ernie.

Wolf then administered a powerful Heimlich to Ernie.

"*Aaaakkkk!*" went Ernie.

"There!" cried Wolf. "Any meat pop out of his mouth?"

"Yeah," I said. "His tongue. About six inches. Thanks much, Wolf. You cleared his throat."

"You feel okay now, big fella?" Wolf asked.

"Aaakkk," Ernie said, nodding his head and smiling tearfully up at Wolf.

"Good thing I took the lifesaving course this morning!" Wolf shouted. "Here I thought it was a waste of my time, and already I saved a life!"

We finished eating, bought $20 worth of antacid tablets, and went back to the boat. Ernie was wearing his crazed look again.

"Think of it this way, Ern," I said. "It could have been worse."

"How?"

"Wolf could have got to the part of the first-aid course that covers mouth-to-mouth resuscitation this morning."

"Aaakkk!" Ernie said.

We gassed up the boat and headed back across the lake. We didn't bother to troll, because the wind had come up and the water was getting a little rough.

"I thought you could feel a storm in your bones," Ernie croaked.

"I can," I said. "My bones are aching like crazy. Now shut up and bail!"

We shot straight in over the bar at the mouth of the river, the prop kissing the gravel but without getting serious.

"Hey, I've got pretty darn good at navigating the bar," I said.

"You should," croaked Ernie. "You had a week's practice this morning!"

Ernie's wife, Marge, was waiting for us at their dock. "How was fishing, guys?"

"Didn't get a bite," I said.

"No excitement, hunh?"

"Naw," I said. "Just the usual. You want to go out again tomorrow, Ern?"

"Sure," he said. "What time?"

"Five sharp."

For Crying Out Loud!

I heard the other day it's now okay for men to cry. Can that be true? Probably is. Seems as if every other week they change another rule on me. It's hard to keep up.

I can't remember the last time I cried, but it had to be sometime before I was eight years old. By age eight I had learned the rule that boys and men aren't supposed to cry. I think Crazy Eddie Muldoon and I picked up this rule from the movies. Roy and Gene and Hoppy never cried, no matter how much they got hurt. A whole herd of cattle could stampede over a movie cowboy and flatten him into a fair imitation of Pizza Supreme, and the pizza would look up and say, "Just a scratch." If a movie cowboy got half his innards shot out, he'd say, "Just a flesh wound." Then he'd climb back on his horse and ride over the top of the Rockies after a bad guy. Movie cowboys were tough. So were Eddie and I.

One day we were cutting steaks off a horse to take on one of our camping trips. Because the horse had been lying dead in the Muldoon pasture for several weeks, we were pretty sure Eddie's pa wouldn't mind if we removed a few steaks from it. We were using Mr. Muldoon's hunting knife, which Eddie had borrowed for the task while his pa was away from home. Had he been there, Mr. Muldoon no doubt would have said, "Why sure, boys, help yourself to any of my razor-sharp knives to cut some steaks off that dead horse." But he wasn't home. Anyway, when it came time for me to slice off a steak, the knife slipped and cut my thumb to the bone.

Right away Eddie looked at my eyes, to see if I was going to violate the code and burst out crying. But I didn't. I wanted to say, "It's just a flesh wound," but I knew that if I unclenched my teeth for even a second I'd go, "Waaaahhhh!" So I tore a piece off my grungy T-shirt, wrapped it around my thumb, and went home without so much as a whimper. Eddie was impressed—heck, *I* was impressed! Eddie was probably a little worried, too, because he knew for sure that no matter how badly he got hurt, at least around me, he could never cry, although, personally, I didn't think Eddie could kick the habit. I was finally one up on him.

Later that summer Eddie and I were playing Lone Ranger and Tonto, and the Lone Ranger got bucked off one of the Muldoon milk cows—Silver—and broke his arm. Tonto was pretty sure the Lone Ranger would have cried, if he hadn't also got the wind knocked out of him. How lucky can a kid get! Later, Eddie made a pretty good case that not crying over a broken arm was a whole lot better than not crying over a measly cut thumb. So he had his edge back.

I was eight years old when I cut my thumb, so I know that any crying I did had to be before then. My tough old pioneer grandmother also put a damper on my crying. Whenever I ran in the house bawling about some injury, she'd say, "Why you big calf!" (Calves bawl—get it? I didn't until I was grown up, but even as a kid I still recognized it as a serious insult to my boyhood.) Womenfolk in those days wouldn't put up with whimpering males. But now, after all these years, they change the rules. When I think of all the times I could have burst out crying and how good it would have made me feel, why, it's just infuriating.

A few years ago, I hooked what was probably the biggest bull trout ever to come out of Lake Koocanusa, except it didn't come out. After gently retrieving the fish from numerous long runs, I finally got it up alongside the boat. My friend Dave leaned over to net it. At that moment, seeing its chance, the fish made a final lunge and cut the line on the prop.

"Wheweee!" Dave said. "That was one monster fish. Too bad it got away."

"Yeah," I said. "Well, that's fishing. There's no guarantee. That's the way the cookie crumbles. What the heck, that's not the only fish in the lake."

But just think. If I'd known the no-crying rule had been rescinded, I could have gone, "Waaahhhhh! I wanted that fish, Dave! Waaaahhhh! It's so unfair! Waaahhh!"

See, I could have expressed my true feelings.

And rather than breaking into a fit of retching, as he would have under the old code, Dave would have said, "That's okay, Pat. You have yourself a good cry. You deserve it. Here, take my hanky."

But nobody had told me the no-crying rule had been rescinded!

I can't count the number of camping trips I've suffered through with feigned hardiness, gumption, and grit. Here's just one example:

Retch Sweeney and I were lying in our two-man tent,

which seemed to be pitched under a waterfall. Rain had been pounding down in torrents for two days. Not only did we have six inches of ice water in the tent, we had actual current! Small icebergs were floating by between our sleeping bags. My body was going numb from cold but not fast enough. "I can still feel my legs!" I shouted. "I can still feel my legs!"

Retch, who has made a hobby of collecting ways to irritate people, had discovered yet another one, as if our predicament weren't miserable enough already.

"I wish we had some jelly beans," he said. "Don't you wish we had some jelly beans?"

"No. I hate jelly beans."

"You don't like jelly beans?"

"No."

"Huh. That's hard to believe. You really don't like jelly beans?"

"I just said I don't like jelly beans!"

"You really mean that? You don't like jelly beans?"

"For the last time, I don't like jelly beans, I can't stand jelly beans, and I never want to hear jelly beans mentioned ever again in my lifetime!"

Silence. After a bit, Retch said, "I guess that means you don't like jelly beans, right? You're not just kidding me? Tell me the truth now, you really don't like jelly beans?"

At this point, if I had known the rule about not crying had been rescinded, I would have burst into tears. As it was, all I could do was hold Retch's head underwater until either he drowned or he forgot about jelly beans, whichever came first.

Think how allowing men to cry will change the rugged sport of elk hunting. A group of elk hunters has been in the saddle for twelve straight hours. In the old days, they'd have been joking about their misery.

"Somebody check my saddle. I think it's on fire! Ha ha."

"Now I know how a turkey wishbone feels at Thanksgiving. Ha ha."

Under the new code, elk hunters can express to their guide how they actually feel: "Waaaaahhh! How much farther to camp, Ed? Waaaahhhh!"

"Only another ten miles. But it's all practically straight up."

"Waaaaaahhhh!"

It was a big relief for me to learn that women now like men who know how to cry. Say you spill some gravy on your new tie at supper. "Oh darn!" you cry. "I just bought this new tie today and already it's ruined, just ruined! Waaaahhh!" And then your wife or girlfriend will say, "Oh, I do so like it when you cry, sweetheart. There, there, you can buy yourself another tie." You smile through your tears, because you really didn't like that tie anyway. Dropping the no-cry rule for males changes the whole relationship between men and women. This is great! No longer do we have to pretend to be rugged, tough, and immune to pain.

When I smashed my thumb with a hammer last week, I decided to try out male crying on my wife, Bun. Instead of doing my usual crouch hop about the yard with hand clutched in my crotch while I defoliated the shrubbery with colorful expressions, something Bun disapproves of, by the way, I rushed into the kitchen bellowing for all I was worth and holding up the injured digit for inspection, a Band-Aid, and possibly a kiss.

"Why, you big calf!" Bun snarled. "Knock that off! Are you trying to make me gag, or what?"

I guess she hadn't got the word yet, that it's now okay for men to cry. Just my luck.

Fan Mail

Every month I receive a dozen or so fan letters from youngsters telling me how much they love my books and requesting that I answer a few questions for them. I must say that it is gratifying to find so many youngsters with such a keen interest in fine literature that they would go to all to the trouble to write their favorite author. Here is a typical example:

Dear Pat:

You are my favorite author and my teacher gave us this assignment to write a letter to our favorite author and then write a report on him and if you don't reply to this letter I get an F on the assignment and I'm sure you wouldn't want that on your conscience. So please answer the 337 questions I have submitted with this letter. I would appreciate it if you would type your reply double space with one-inch margins but allow enough room at the top of the page for me to add a title, my name, and a couple of comments of my own on my report. Please send your reply by one-day mail, as my assignment is due at the end of this week.

Your devoted fan,
Donald

P.S. As soon as I get an answer to my letter, I promise that I will actually read one of your books, and I mean that sincerely.

Here is my typical reply:

Dear Donald:

Thank you very much for the nice letter. I was pleased to learn that I am your favorite author. Because I must spend most of my time hunting and fishing and generally having a lot of fun—and no longer must attend school like you, ha ha!—and also because of your pressing deadline, I can answer only a few of your questions. Here goes:

Question 14: How old are you?

Answer: Age 37.

Question 22: Are your stories true or do you make them up?

Answer: They are all true. One of my principles is never to tell lies. Lying is a disgusting habit and one that I hope you will avoid. If I may be so bold as to say so, Donald, it would be a good idea for you to model your life after my own, one of integrity, high principle, temperance in all things, and rigid adherence to the unvarnished truth.

Question 41: I think the funniest story you ever wrote is "Grandma and the Buck Deer." Is that one of your favorites, too?

Answer: No, it is not! I think it is a stupid and disgust-

ing story and certainly does not deserve the literary reputation and acclaim that it has earned over the years, and I
would hold to that opinion even if I had written that story
instead of an author by the name of Joel Vance. Mr. Vance
has authored a book by the same title, and I suggest you
take pains to avoid it. A great many people have written
over the years to congratulate me on my having authored
"Grandma and the Buck Deer," which goes to show the
dismal state into which literary taste in this country has
fallen. I must tell you, Donald, that there is no story ever
written that I have grown to detest more.

Question 63: What kind of gun do you use for hunting
grizzly bears?

Answer: A big one. Preferably one that I can shoot back
over my shoulder while moving at a fast pace. I must admit
that I don't hunt grizzlies anymore, now that I have given
up the bow and arrow. I only wish grizzlies would regard
our relationship the same way as I—neither of us hunts the
other. A grizzly lives on the mountain where I do my daily
hiking. I refuse to allow a mere grizzly to dictate to me
where I can or cannot hike, although I am open to any sug-
gestions he might care to make. On a couple of occasions a
gray stump has reared up out of the brush and propelled
me into the upper branches of a pine tree for a better view
of it. Gray stumps can be deadly, particularly during twilight, and every year are responsible for a number of heart
failures in grizzly country. My friend Retch Sweeney was
recently chased for nearly a mile by a gray stump. Fortunately, he managed to escape unharmed, but the stump
pretty much ended his career as a wilderness hunting guide.

Question 154: Do you like—yuck!—girls?

Answer: What a strange question! It was once popular
with army psychiatrists, but comes unexpected from a boy
your age. Of course I like girls! When I was your age, or
perhaps a little younger, my view of girls was basically that

they occupied space that might better be used for something else, like potted plants. As I grew older, however, I became increasingly fond of them, until at last I wandered into that vast wilderness that is love and have been lost in it ever since. If only I'd had the good sense to leave a trail of bread crumbs to find my way out!

Question 189: Have you ever had an out-of-body experience?

Answer: Yes, I have, Donald. One day I was studying a piece of rock in my hand. It seemed familiar. Then I realized it was the very same rock that was supposed to be holding me to the side of a cliff. As I plummeted toward the ground below, my whole life flashed before my eyes, which I took to be a bad omen, even if it was a rerun. I don't remember hitting the ground, but a short while later I experienced the sensation of expanding and expanding and becoming lighter and lighter and then floating up into the air. At first, I thought it might merely be a result of the green hash we'd eaten for breakfast that morning. But then I looked down, and there were my fishing companions, Retch Sweeney and Al Finley, crouched over a flattened, prostrate figure more or less shaped like a gingerbread man. And it was *me!* Gave me a bit of a start, I can tell you that, Donald. It was the first time my body and I had ever been separated. Then I heard Al say, "I think we've lost him, Retch," and Retch nodded sadly. "No!" I yelled down at them. "I'm not lost yet! Look up here, you fools!" But they didn't seem to hear me. Then Retch became all panicky and started yelling almost hysterically. As I recall, he was yelling that if he and Al didn't stop fooling around and hurry up, they would get to Moose Lake too late to fish. Suddenly, I felt very angry, possibly because Retch and Al were arguing over how to divide up my gear, and all at once I was sucked back into my body, which was pretty darn glad to see me, too.

Question 204: What's the biggest fish you've ever caught?

Answer: About this big, Donald. Maybe even a little bigger.

Question 205: What's the biggest elk you've ever shot?

Answer: About this big, Donald. Maybe even a little bigger.

Question 243: What is the ideal hunting vehicle?

Answer: Any vehicle belonging to someone else.

Question 267: What is the ideal outdoor companion?

Answer: An excellent question, Donald! This is why it is so important to select your friends carefully. Always avoid relationships with individuals who display any sort of habits unacceptable in polite society, unless, of course, they happen to own a late-model hunting vehicle. Some individuals are so gross, however, that even their possession of a good hunting vehicle is not enough. In that case, one should avoid associating with them no matter what they might own, the one exception being a fine hunting dog. Anyone who owns a fine hunting dog can't be all that bad. I should point out here that my friend Retch Sweeney owns both a good hunting vehicle and a fine hunting dog, just in case you were wondering, Donald. Retch's character is still borderline, but I hear he just bought a jet boat for fishing on the Snake River, and if that is true, I believe he will have acquired the moral, ethical, and social qualities one generally finds in the ideal outdoor companion.

Question 273: How long have you been writing professionally?

Answer: Almost exactly forty years. You may detect a minor disparity between the number of years I've been writing and my age as given above. So?

Question 285: Why did you become a writer?

Answer: I am frequently asked that same question, Donald, usually by my wife, Bun. It is impossible here to indicate the exact tone of voice in which Bun asks the question, but it is such that I am fairly certain she does not merely wish to satisfy her curiosity. Basically, the answer is: it was either that or go to work. Not that writing isn't hard work. It merely seems to be easy to the outside observer. For example, I may be down at Kelly's Bar & Grill shooting a few games of pool and smoking a cigar and laughing and joking with the guys, but the truth is, I'm really hard at work writing. Inside my brain, where writing actually takes place, I'm just this churning cauldron of work, with my brain gasping and wheezing and sweating and crying out from its incredible exertion. But then, when I go home and flop down in front of the television to give my brain a little rest and relaxation and entertainment, you would be surprised how difficult it is to explain to my spouse that I haven't merely been frittering away an afternoon in a sleazy pool hall. So, writing is not an easy life, Donald, no indeed.

Question 300: Do you have to be extremely intelligent to be a writer?

Answer: Yes. Also, you need to be extremely well educated. I myself spent nine years at the university, several of those years as a sophomore. In fact, some of my professors took to referring to me as McManus the Sophomore. I majored in English and minored in philosophy. I minored in philosophy in order to figure out why I was majoring in English. At the time, there were still jobs available for English majors, but two of my classmates got hired for them. So there was nothing left for me to do but to go into writing. If you decide to become an English major, Donald, always abbreviate it as "Eng." That way your parents might think you are majoring in engineering and will one day amount to something, and that they aren't throwing their money away to help you become one of the few people in the world who can distinguish a gerund from a participle.

Question 308: Do you have an extra .410 shotgun lying around that you will send to me?

Answer: No.

Question 310: Have you ever been lost?

Answer: "Lost" is a relative term, Donald. If you are asking if I have ever spent three days and nights in the woods looking for where I left my car, the answer is yes.

If you are asking whether search-and-rescue parties have combed the mountains looking for me, the answer is yes.

If you are asking if I have ever taken a shortcut over a mountain pass in Montana and ended up knocking on a door in a small town somewhere in Canada, the answer is yes. But if you are asking if I've ever been actually lost, the answer is no. The truth is, I have a superb sense of direction, even to the extent of proving compasses wrong.

Question 318: Do sporting goods manufacturers send you all kinds of neat equipment free so that you can test it and promote it for them on television?

Answer: No, they don't. It is true that most other outdoor writers get a lot of neat free stuff to test, but not me. Even when a manufacturer hears that I've *bought* a piece of his equipment, a representative will show up and try to buy it back from me, often at double what I paid for it! Sporting goods manufacturers have absolutely no regard for my feelings.

Well, Donald, that is all the time I have for answering your questions. Now I must get busy and write another column for *Outdoor Life,* provided that the Board of Health hasn't shut down Kelly's Bar & Grill yet again.

Your favorite author,
Pat

Bike Ride

It was said of the Huns who conquered Rome, "Their country is the back of a horse." (And a sorry country it must have been, too, or so I judge from my own experience on the backs of horses.) In the days of my youth, if not today, it similarly could have been said of boys, "Their country is the back of a bicycle." We lived on our bikes. These one-wheel-drive, all-terrain vehicles transported us to our hunting, fishing, camping, and swimming, and indeed, to adventures too numerous to extract from memory. In fact, the mere act of riding my bike could count as an adventure, and a harrowing one at that. I now regard that old bike with a certain degree of fondness, but only because the passage of much time has erased the fear and loathing I once felt for that misbegotten piece of mechanical malevolence. If a machine could be possessed by evil spirits, I'd have nominated my bike as a prime candidate for exorcism.

After I had grown up and had children of my own, I bought them all shiny new bicycles, which were never available as a means of transportation, because they were busy accumulating dust in the back of the garage. As most parents are aware these days, Mom or Pop and the family car are now a child's preferred means of travel from one place to another. When I as a boy suggested to my own parents that they drive me to a friend's house and later retrieve me, they dissolved into such an unseemly state of mirth that I could not help but consider myself one of the world's great wits.

"Did"—*wheeze*—"did you hear what Patrick just said?"

"Yes! Drive him over to"—*gasp*—"Lester's house!"

"And actually return later to . . . !"

"Oh, stop, stop! No more! My sides ache!"

Once their spasms of hilarity had subsided, my mother would ask, "And what's wrong with your bike?"

What was wrong with my bike? Well, let's see. First of all, it was not store bought. Its parts had been cannibalized from assorted wreckage of other bicycles and then assembled by a sadistic local handyman, who must have chortled evilly all through the process of creating the two-wheeled monster. The seat, apparently salvaged from a racing model, was slightly less comfortable than riding about on a hatchet head—bystanders sometimes thought I was *yodeling* when I shot by them on my way home from a long day's ride. ("Better work on that yodel, kid!")

Because the seat was permanently fixed at a height unsuited to my short legs, I could reach the pedals only with my toes. ("You'll grow into it.") The front wheel had a habit of bouncing off, a malfunction that would have flipped me over the handlebars, except by then the chain would have eaten my pants leg in order to prevent me from ejecting before the crash. By the end of the typical summer, I looked like a poster child for bike safety: "Kids, ride carefully. Don't let *this* happen to you!" And Mom had the audacity to ask me what was wrong with my bike.

The bike was equipped with coaster brakes, the only kind of bicycle brakes available at the time, as far as I know. My brakes never seemed to work properly, and so one day I decided to undertake their repair. As it turned out, the brakes consisted of what seemed to be a series slotted steel washers, which upon removal from their shaft immediately became a glob of slotted steel washers on the ground. I reassembled them as best I could, carefully wiping off most of the dirt and grass, but with the panicky sensation that I had succeeded only in destroying my sole means of transportation. And the panicky sensation was right on. I now had a bike that was still serviceable, except in any situation where I needed to stop.

There was nothing to do but empty out my life's savings and take the bike back for a brake job to the sadist who had built it in the first place, Mr. Eli Croaker. Unfortunately, Mr. Croaker's shop was located at his farm atop a long steep hill on the highway that led through the main street of town. One warm September Saturday, I trudged up the mile-long hill, pushing the bike. When I finally arrived at the farm, a pack of mangy dogs rushed out to see if I might be edible, but I managed to fend them off with a few well-aimed kicks as I pounded on the shop door. No response. I then tried the farmhouse. Still no response. I wandered about calling, "Mr. Croaker! Mr. Croaker! Are you home?" Silence. My exhausting hike up the hill had been in vain.

I plopped down on the house porch, wishing I had paid

more attention to my stepfather's vocabulary when he mashed his thumb with a hammer, because I could have used some of those colorful expressions at the moment. They had seemed to improve Hank's mood considerably, and my own mood was in serious need of improvement. As I sat there recuperating for the trek back down the hill, I suddenly noticed a movement in the woods on the far side of the highway. What a stroke of luck! My cousin Buck and his two cronies, Red Higgins and Sid Lasky, soon emerged from the trees and began urgently tromping in my direction, each carrying a shotgun. They'd been out grouse hunting. Surely they had driven a car up to the top of the hill and could give me and my bike a ride home.

"What you doin' here?" Buck greeted me. He was several years older than I and twice as big. He had a job and a car and all kinds of neat stuff that I could use anytime I wanted, as long as Buck was safely at work. He had recently reached the age where he knew everything worth knowing. He often told me so himself, so I knew it was true. Later, he would turn out to be only slightly smarter than celery, but at this age, he knew just about everything.

I started to explain my predicament. "Well, my bike—"

"Forget the bike. Where's ole Croaker?"

"He's not home. My bike—"

"Drat! Wanted to bum a drink of water off him. We're dying of thirst."

Red pointed down at the town far below. "Man, I can see Lulu's Drive-In from here. All those icy drinks just waiting for us, but so far away, so far away. Aiiigh! I can't stand it!"

"Don't even talk about it," Sid rasped. "Otherwise, I'll have to shoot you."

"I'll be dead of thirst by the time we walk all the way to Lulu's," Buck croaked, staring down at the drive-in, faint and tiny in the distance.

"You didn't bring a car?" I said.

"No, stupid, we didn't bring a car," Buck said in his mimicky voice. "We hunted up the other side of the mountain, and . . ." He stopped. He was studying my bike.

"Wait a minute," he said. "I think I'll just hop on Patrick's bike and coast down the hill. Be at Lulu's in no time! Hot dang!"

"But, Buck, my bike—"

"Don't get your tail in a knot. I'll pay you a whole dollar for the use of it."

"But, Buck, my bike—"

"Oh, all right, you miserable little rat, two dollars! And not a penny more!"

"Deal!"

"Hey, wait a minute," Red said. "How about me?"

"You can ride on the back-fender carrier," Buck said. "But it'll cost you a dollar."

"Hey, no way, you guys," Sid whined. "I ain't walking down the hill by myself!"

"Well, then, get on the handlebars," Buck said. "It ain't like I'll have to pedal. Cost you a dollar, though, Sid."

Buck was always a shrewd businessman. He wasn't even out of the yard yet, and he'd already made back his investment.

They stashed their guns and game bags in Mr. Croaker's woodshed, and climbed on the bike. That's when I had a terrifying thought. Suppose they crashed and had to spend weeks in the hospital and Buck would lose his job and . . . ! It was time for me to speak out.

"Hold up a second, Buck," I yelled.

Buck twisted around and glared at me. "What now?"

"Pay me my two dollars *first!*"

Buck dug out the two bills Red and Sid had just given him and graciously threw them on the ground. Then the three of them wobbled out to the highway, hit the down slope, and glided away, gradually picking up speed.

"Lulu's, here we come!" shouted Red.

"Hoo boy!" yelled Sid from his precarious perch on the handlebars. "Here we—uh, better slow up a bit, Buck! I said, slo—OOOOOOOoooooo . . . ooo . . . oo . . . o . . . !"

I lost sight of them after they careened around the first curve, but reports from various eyewitnesses drifted about town for months and even years afterward. The reports improved considerably with age.

Wally Hedge said he was thinking of buying a used motorcycle and was out testing it to see what it would do, when three guys shot past him on a bicycle. Disgusted, Wally immediately returned the motorcycle to its owner.

Old Mrs. Wiggens, who was driving up the hill at the time, reported that when the bike went into the last curve before it hit the straightaway into town, Buck and Red were both skidding their feet along the pavement. She said she wasn't sure if their boots were actually on fire but they were trailing wisps of smoke.

About the time the bike reached the town limits, Fred Perkins heard a loud noise, or so he claimed in later years, after he'd learned about sonic booms caused by objects passing through the sound barrier.

Ed Cominskey had just ordered another beer at Billy's Tavern when he glanced out into Main Street. "Better hold that last beer, Billy," he said. "Either I'm hallucinating or three fellows just buzzed Main Street on a bicycle. Weren't no more than a foot off the pavement!"

The raucous teenaged crowd at Lulu's Drive-In fell into stunned silence after the bike streaked past. Then Lulu said, "Wasn't that Sid Lasky on the handlebars? It looked kinda like Sid."

"Naw," one of the kids said. "That guy was at least fifty years old. Couldn't be Sid."

"You'd think an old guy like that would know better," Lulu said. "Riding on handlebars at his age! My word!"

"Well, the guy on the seat wasn't much younger," someone else said. "But I'll say this for him—he can sure pedal a bike!"

The bike finally coasted to a stop on the far side of town. Its occupants escaped unscathed from their ride, except for Sid, who had the imprints of several large flying insects embedded in his forehead, kind of like a human fossil. It was neat. I would have liked to take Sid to school and enter him as my science project. Buck said later that for a while he thought they might have to have Sid surgically removed from the handlebars, but after a while Sid relaxed a little, and Buck and Red were able to peel him off without too much trouble.

Buck, Sid, and Red came over to my house that evening and asked my mother to send me out. They said they just wanted to return my bike and thank me for the loan of it. But I made it over the back fence and into the woods before they had a chance to show their appreciation.

Uncle Flynn's
Hairy Adventure

I have recently been thinking about shaving off my beard. My reason for growing a beard in the first place is a bit obscure to me now, but I'm sure it was a good one. Some of my associates probably think I grew it because the beard makes me almost indistinguishable from Ernest Hemingway, even though they are careful not to mention that striking resemblance. Their silence on the matter clearly arises out of jealousy. My former friend Fenton Quagmire once observed that I reminded him of a famous writer who lived in Paris during the 1920s.

"Ernest Hemingway?" I suggested.

"No, Gertrude Stein! Ha!"

So, there is yet another example of jealousy rearing its ugly head.

Growing a beard is not something to be undertaken

lightly. For at least the first three weeks of the process you go about looking as though you haven't shaved for three weeks, which is, of course, the case. So you feel compelled to explain your unseemly appearance to anyone you meet.

"I'm growing a beard," you casually explain to each person you encounter. Typical responses:

"Yes sir. Now, did you want the soup or the salad with your dinner?"

"Bully for you, sir. Now, if you'll show me your driver's license, perhaps we can discuss why you were doing forty in a twenty-five-mile-an-hour zone."

"That's real nice, guy. Now do as I asked. Hand over your wallet and watch so we can get this robbery completed."

To counter the impression that you're a hobo waiting for the next empty boxcar out of town, you are forced into wearing a suit and tie everywhere you go, and even that doesn't help much when it comes to cashing checks. The picture on your driver's license is of a clean-shaven person.

"I'm growing a beard," you explain to the clerk.

"It certainly can't hurt," she replies, staring at the license photo.

Many people hate beards. My own mother was one of those people. During my bohemian days in graduate school, I grew a really nice shaggy beard and then made the mistake of going home during spring break. Mom met me at the door and let out such a shriek I thought someone had sneaked up behind me with an ax.

"You shave that disgusting thing off this instant!" she exclaimed by way of greeting.

Mom loudly expressed her belief that only a man who didn't have a job and never intended to get one would grow a beard.

"So?" I said.

Every time I came into the house, even though I had been away only five minutes, Mom would greet me with the words, "What! You haven't shaved off that disgusting thing yet?" Mom was a third-degree black belt in nagging. Bit by bit, she started to wear me down, particularly with the phrase "that disgusting thing." I started to feel as if I had a huge, hairy spider attached to my face. I fought back, offering up examples of great men who had worn beards.

"Abraham Lincoln wore a beard, Mom."

"Yes, and look what happened to him!"

So much for the logical approach. Finally, I could stand it no longer. Nothing is worth causing a mother such anguish. She probably was lying awake nights fretting about my beard. Maybe she was afraid her friends would see me and offer their condolences over the way her son had turned out. Maybe she thought people would point to her on the street. "There goes the woman whose son wears a beard," they'd say. Banks would refuse to approve loans for anyone in the family. Bankruptcy would result. We'd all be destitute. Hurricanes, earthquakes, and volcanic eruptions would follow, soon to be joined by the four horsemen of the Apocalypse. I went into the bathroom and shaved off my beard.

Thinking Mom's joyous cries at the sight of my clean-shaven face would be reward enough for the loss of my beloved beard, I walked into the kitchen. "Look, Mom. Notice anything different about me?"

She studied me closely for a moment. "Well, you could certainly use a haircut."

Is it any wonder the field of psychotherapy flourishes?

Nearly all male writers wear beards. We have many uses for them, most of which escape me at the moment. They do come in handy for fly tying, of course, and also for collecting insect samples on trout streams. At one time, the beards of us writers served to express our rugged individualism and helped to distinguish us from people who had actual jobs. That is no longer the case. Nowadays, corporate presidents are showing up at the office wearing their vacation-grown beards. I even have a banker friend who wears a full beard but is still regarded among his business associates as a highly respected and responsible leader in the world of finance. My mother, of course, wouldn't deposit so much as a dime in his bank until he shaved off that disgusting thing.

My wife, Bun, theorizes that the primary purpose of a beard is concealment of a weak chin, multiple chins, or even multiple weak chins. I don't know how she comes up with such nonsense. Bun did comment awhile back that she thought I looked good in a beard. "You kind of remind me of one of those famous writers who lived in Paris back in the twenties."

"I'm not falling for that one again," I said.

It might be thought that a beard brings a degree of efficiency to personal hygiene in that it saves all the time otherwise devoted to shaving. Nothing could be further from the truth. Wearing a beard is not too much different from wearing a small garden on your face. Without hours of devoted care, it soon gets away from its owner, becomes overgrown, and spreads out over the surrounding landscape. That is what happened to my Uncle Flynn and ultimately led to the unfortunate event that is still recalled with glee among the more malicious members of our family.

My mother used to refer to this particular period of family history as the time her brother Flynn was so much sought after. "Oh, Flynn is much sought after," she'd say. She allowed it to be assumed that it was employers who sought after Flynn, but that was not really the case. The persons seeking after him were usually some of his gambling associates, and probably also the law, although I'm not sure about the law.

Uncle Flynn holed up in a mountain cabin for most of one winter, apparently for the purpose of lowering the risk of unexpected encounters with some of his fellow gamblers. It was during this sabbatical from his chosen profession that he grew a beard. Also about this time, Uncle Flynn developed a back problem, a malady of great puzzlement to all of us, because the heaviest thing Flynn ever lifted was a pool cue or a deck of cards. If he reached down to pick up something off the floor, his back would get a catch in it. Bent over and with arms hanging akimbo, a posture not unlike that of an ape, he would howl with pain. Mom, rather unsympathetically it seemed to me, said she thought Flynn's bad back must have resulted from his accidentally getting too close to a job and dislocating a vertebra when he leaped back in fear and loathing.

Uncle Flynn started the beard, as I understood at the time, more or less as a hobby, there being little else in the way of entertainment at the cabin. He tried various styles, trimming and shaping this way and that, until at last he tired of the hobby and simply let the beard grow as it saw fit. Black, curly foliage quickly engulfed both sides and the lower half of his face and then descended in wild abandon down his chest. Flynn found some amusement from time to time in measuring the length of his beard, but not enough. After studying in a mirror the transformation he had undergone from a dapper man-about-town to something resembling the Wild Man of Borneo, he suddenly realized that he might very well escape recognition if he were to slip into town after dark and take in a movie at the Pandora Theater. And that is what he did, augmenting his disguise with an old pair of bib overalls, a tattered flannel shirt, and a grungy mackinaw that had served to plug up a hole in the cabin wall.

Uncle Flynn waited until the theater lights had gone down and the newsreel had begun before buying his ticket and popcorn and finding a seat in the darkened theater. By great good fortune, or so Flynn thought at the time, the seat he selected turned out to be right next to that of Miss Sarah Jane Trillabee, the town librarian and a woman of somewhat stern personality, but otherwise not unattractive.

Flynn's attention soon drifted from the movie, *Frankenstein Meets the Wolfman,* to Miss Trillabee. Forgetting that he was no longer his usual dapper self, Flynn offered the librarian some of his popcorn. She refused with a curt shake of her head, obviously being of the impression that ill fate had seated a tramp right next to her. Unaccustomed to rebuffs from women, Flynn now felt challenged. As the movie progressed, he'd lean over from time to time and whisper some witty comment about activities on the screen. The librarian grew increasingly incensed by the provocations of the hairy creature next to her. Finally, she'd had enough. She thrust her arms into her coat sleeves, arose in a huff, and began to squeeze her way past Flynn. Then it happened. For a brief instant, Miss Trillabee momentarily lost her balance and fell against the source of her ire. Startled by Miss Trillabee's sudden effort to flee his attentions, Flynn tried to rise and draw his legs out of her way but was momentarily pinned in his seat as she fell against him.

Except for one of those unlucky coincidences that always seemed to overtake Flynn, it is likely the situation would have been resolved simply by Miss Trillabee's complaining to the manager and the manager asking Flynn to stop annoying the other patrons, or, in the extreme, refunding the price of his ticket and ordering him from the theater. What happened instead, however, serves as an excellent example of the dangers inherent in beards.

Even as Miss Trillabee thrust against Uncle Flynn, she was angrily pulling her coat belt tight around her and snapping shut its clasp. The belt, as Uncle Flynn explained years later, consisted of a web of decorative metal links rather than a simple cloth affair, which could not possibly have become entangled with a curly beard. Alas, as the clasp of the belt snapped shut, Uncle Flynn found his face painfully and hopelessly attached to the back of the town librarian.

Miss Trillabee, of course, had not so much as an inkling that she had snagged Uncle Flynn by the beard. Thus, when Flynn grabbed her around the hips with both hands and pulled her back into his face, trying desperately to get some slack in his beard, she could not help but misinterpret his actions or his intent.

"Stop that, you crazy fool!" she hissed over her shoulder at the hunched form of her assailant. She twisted sharply around trying to get a shot at Flynn with her purse, a tactic that flung Uncle Flynn out into the aisle but still not free of her belt. It was at this moment that the audience heard, as later reported in the Blight *Bugle,* a sound very much like the anguished howl of a wolf. The catch in Flynn's back had caught! For a second or two, the audience supposed the howl had come from the movie, but this supposition was soon erased by a piercing scream from Miss Trillabee, the result of Flynn's clawing frantically at her backside in an effort to undo his beard. Instantly, the house lights went up.

What the nearest members of the audience then observed, even as they blinked in the sudden luminosity, was Uncle Flynn crouched in the aisle with his face pressed against the rear of the librarian.

"Here, you!" a man shouted. "Stop that, you fiend!"

Several men arose from their seats, ready to charge to the aid of a lady in distress. But even as he had been flung howling into the aisle, Uncle Flynn had hit upon a desperate solution to the predicament—he would cut his beard loose from the belt with his pocket knife. He released his hold on Miss Trillabee just long enough to extract and open his knife.

"Watch out!" someone shouted. "The tramp's got a knife!"

As might be expected, this mention of a knife had less than a calming effect on the librarian's would-be rescuers, and much less so on Miss Trillabee herself. She immediately ceased her flailing with purse and bolted up the aisle, through the lobby, and out of the theater, all the while closely pursued by Flynn. Realizing at this point that she still hadn't shaken off the crazed and lecherous tramp, Miss Trillabee suddenly stopped and concentrated her efforts on purse flailing and language most inappropriate for a librarian. It was then Flynn managed to cut loose his beard from the belt. He fled up the street and disappeared into the darkness behind Grogan's War Surplus.

According to the Blight *Bugle*, some men from the audience had rather tentatively followed Miss Trillabee and her knife-wielding assailant from the theater, where they observed that the tramp had scurried off very much like an ape, all hunched over and with arms hanging akimbo. Several witnesses expressed concern over whether Miss Trillabee's assailant had been human at all, because minutes after he—or it—had vanished into the night, they heard from off in the distance a howl so eerie and haunting that one man said it was enough to make your flesh crawl.

When the Blight *Bugle* came out and we read about the horrible incident at the Pandora Theater, we were naturally

shocked, but never for a moment did we make any connection with Flynn. A few days later, Mom took some food
and clean clothes up to the cabin where Uncle Flynn had
holed up. She reported upon her return that Flynn had become terribly irritable when she started to tell him about
the Pandora thing, and had even shouted out, "Stop! Stop!
I don't want to hear!" Mom said she thought his lack of excitement in recent months was starting to get on his nerves.
"And he simply will not stop complaining about his silly
back! My goodness, you'd think he actually used it."

"Maybe Uncle Flynn should go into town and see a
chiropractor," I suggested.

"That's rather unwise, if you ask me. You know, Flynn
is much sought after."

"I know," I said. "But I don't think anyone will recognize him with his beard."

"Oh, Flynn shaved off that disgusting thing," she said.
"He could certainly use a haircut, though."

Hunting the Wily Avid

No greater bond exists between two male friends than shared ignorance. It's wonderful. Shared knowledge is fine as far as it goes, but one friend invariably knows more about a given topic than the other, thereby creating an intellectual imbalance. Shared ignorance, on the other hand, provides for perfect equilibrium. It is limitless. There is no end of topics for conversation based on mutual ignorance.

I have several really good pals with whom I share ignorance. We converse for hours about subjects we know nothing about. With most of my friends, actual knowledge about a topic would lead to either very short conversations or even arguments that might grow bitter and ultimately destroy a friendship.

"Why, that's not true."

"Who says?"

"I say."

"Let's look it up in the *Guinness Book of World Records*. There, see, I'm right, you moron! Ha ha ha ha!"

Arguments like that never arise when two friends enjoy shared ignorance of a topic.

"You know what's causin' all these earthquakes? It's that hole in the ozone."

"You're right about that. It's lettin' in too much gravity."

"Gravity, yeah, way too much of it. Gravity keeps buildin' up and buildin' up, and pretty soon you got your earthquakes."

"You're right about that, ol' buddy."

If either friend knew anything at all about holes in ozone, gravity, or earthquakes, he would be under an unrestrained compulsion to reveal this bit of knowledge, and the conversation would abruptly end. Furthermore, an element of distrust would enter the relationship, because one of the friends would feel insecure in happily discoursing away on a topic he knows absolutely nothing about. He would be in constant fear of exposing his ignorance to assault by an actual thought or fact.

Eighty-seven percent of all conversations between friends are based on shared ignorance. It's true. That's the reason so many friendships last a lifetime. There is even a procedure for testing a friend's ignorance on a topic, to see if it matches your own. It goes something like this.

"George, you know anything about the national debt?"

"Naw. You?"

"Naw. But I'll tell you what causes it. Too much gravity."

"You got that right, ol' buddy."

After running their little test on shared ignorance, the two friends can then discourse in mutual confidence on a topic about which neither of them knows the slightest thing.

My friend Retch Sweeney and I have spent many a happy hour around the campfire sharing our mutual ignorances. Just about any topic will do for the evening, because Retch is a vast reservoir of ignorance. His only academic achievement—a record—was Most Years in Fifth Grade. As my friend, he feels totally confident and secure in his ignorance. He can go on at impressive length discussing the nuances of a subject he never even heard of until the moment it came up.

"You hear that fellow talking about the chaos theory on the radio just now?"

"Yeah."

"You know anything about the chaos theory?"

"Naw. You?"

"Naw. But I'll tell you somethin' about chaos."

"Got anything to do with the hole in the ozone?"

"How'd you guess?"

As I've indicated, the problem with ignorance arises when it isn't shared equally among friends discussing a particular topic. This can put a heavy strain on a relationship. Here's an example.

It all started when I was being interviewed on our local radio station. At one point, the interviewer said, "What do you do for recreation, Pat?"

"Well, besides fishing, I'm an avid hunter," I replied.

A little later in the day, Retch and I were walking down the street to shop for some new tackle at Lou's Sporting Goods.

"I heard you bein' interviewed on the radio this morning," Retch said.

"How'd I do?" I said.

"Fine. But what was that about you being an avid hunter, you big liar? Ha!"

"What are you talking about, Retch? You know I'm an avid hunter."

"Don't think you can pull that on me. There ain't no such thing as avids."

We walked along in silence for a while. Clearly, Retch's comment revealed a deep chasm in our usual mutual ignorance. Because of our long friendship, I wrestled for a moment with my conscience. I won.

"There are too avids," I said. "I've hunted them for years."

"You have not. I hunt with you all the time an' I've never once seen you hunt avids."

"That's because you're never around during avid season."

"Listen, if there was such a critter as an avid, I'd have heard of it."

"Well, I'm surprised you haven't. Avid hunting is very popular."

Retch chuckled. "You're just foolin' with me."

We came to Kelly's Bar & Grill, the cultural center of our little town of Blight, Idaho.

"You think I'm fooling with you, Retch? Why then, you just step into Kelly's here for a minute."

We stepped into Kelly's.

"Gentlemen, gentlemen!" I called out to the Kelly's regulars. "I'm running a little study for the Fish and Game Department. Would every man here who's an avid hunter raise his hand?"

Hands went up all over the room.

"You see," I said to Retch. "Avid hunting is a popular sport. There are probably more avid hunters than all the deer and elk hunters combined."

"Well, if that don't beat all," Retch said. "Seems as if everybody but me has hunted avids for years."

"Seems that way."

"You don't have to be so smug about it."

"I'm not being smug. I just get this urge to smile at strange times."

"What do these avids look like anyway? Maybe I've seen them and didn't know what they was."

"What does an avid look like? You want to know what an avid looks like, Retch?"

"Ain't that what I just said?"

"Right. Let's see now, well, your average avid is about as big as a bread box. Covered with fur. Big ears. Little squinty eyes."

"Good to eat?"

"About like chicken."

"I figured that. How you hunt them?"

"You hunt avids mostly at night. You crouch down and hold a gunnysack open on the ground. When an avid comes along, you shine a flashlight into the sack. The avid sees the light and runs right into the sack. It's pretty simple. Of course, sometimes you have to wait quite a while for an avid to show up. You might want to try it tonight."

Retch's eyes began to narrow into slits, similar to the eyes of an avid right after it has run into a sack.

"I suppose," he growled, "that while you're waiting for an avid to show up you might catch a few snipe in your sack."

"A frequent occurrence," I said. "An avid hunt and a snipe hunt have great similarities."

Retch was pretty steamed. This, after all, had been a classic violation of the bonds of ignorance. I hoped he wouldn't be so upset by my little joke that our enjoyment of shared ignorance would be forever lost.

We walked along without talking for several minutes. Then Retch broke the silence.

"You know anything about the national debt?" he said.

"Naw," I said. "You?"

"Naw. But I'll tell you something, the big problem with the national debt is . . ."

The following stories appeared in *Outdoor Life:*

"The Boy," originally published as "For Whom the Boy Toils," May 1996; "Mountain Men," published in three parts: "Something Bad Blowing on the Wind," June/July 1997, "Caught!," August 1997, and "Pay Back," September 1997; "Smoke!," as "My Stinky Old Pipes," December 1994; "Sam Spud and the Case of the Maltese Fly," May 1997; "Other Than That, Bostich . . . ," as "Littering the Wilds," January 1996; "The Chicken-Fried Club," as "A Glistening Retreat," March 1996; "Into the Twilight, Endlessly Grousing," as "A Good Grouse Woods," November 1995; "Dream Fish," as "Fish of Dreams," April 1996; "Will," as "Where There's a Will," October 1996; "Crime Wave," February 1997; "Big Ben," August 1995; "Roast Beef," as "Midnight Rendezvous," August 1996; "The Fly Rod," March 1997; "The Stupidity Alarm," April 1997; "Work and Other Horrors," June 1994; "The Dangers of Light Tackle," June 1995; "Faint Heart," September 1995; "Mrs. Peabody II," as "R.I.P.," July 1996; "Cereal Crime," as "Sid Is on the Case," October 1994; "Pickers," as "The Competition," December 1995; "My Fishing Trip with Ernie," September 1994; "For Crying Out Loud!," as "Sensitivity Training," January 1997; "Fan Mail," July 1995; "Bike Ride," December 1996; "Uncle Flynn's Hairy Adventure," as "Uncle Finn's Hairy Escape," April 1995; "Hunting the Wily Avid," May 1995.

"Attack of the Stamp People" appeared in *Storyworks,* September 1996.